COME ON DOWN!

# COME ON DOWN!

## Behind the Big Doors at

## Stan Blits

HARPER ENTERTAINMENT
NEW YORK . LONDON . TORONTO . SYDNEY

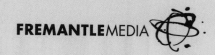

Archive photographs courtesy of CBS Broadcasting, Inc.

FIRST EDITION

*Designed by Timothy Shaner, nightanddaydesign.biz*

Library of Congress Cataloging-in-Publication Data is available upon request.

ISBN: 978-0-06-135011-5
ISBN-10: 0-06-135011-7

07  08  09  10  11  ID/RRD  10  9  8  7  6  5  4  3  2  1

To my father and mother, who, even though horrified by the prospect of my going into a creative field, never flinched, and backed me all the way so I could live my dreams.

# Acknowledgments

Most viewers of television don't care when the credits roll by. That's why TV credits fly across the screen faster than the display on an out-of-control slot machine. Well, now's the time to give credit where credit is due, and in slooooooow motion. Mull over them. Embrace them. Peruse leisurely as you've never been able to before.

All these folks have been amazing during this whole painstaking and exciting process, because they all had something vital and fascinating to contribute to this book, and while I was running around doing other things, these people were doing something for me. I thank them all for being excited for me, believing in me, and supporting me in this lightning-fast journey both on paper and in career. In as many ways as I can say it:

*Thank you, gracias, merci, dank u, danke, toda, arigatou, grazie, qa tlho!*

BOB BARKER: For having the incomparable talent to entertain us for so many years, and thus making it possible for me to share the stories of this show with his gracious support. NORA WONG: For almost killing herself to get this book done and making it her baby. CHUCK HUREWITZ: For his calm, cheerful legal and moral support and patience with a new author. ROGER DOBKOWITZ: For opening the doors to get this done, in addition to his vast knowledge of the show's history. SUE MACINTYRE: For moving heaven and dollar to get me what I needed . . . always. KATHY GRECO: For her fact-digging and enthusiastic moral support in the midst of trying to do her real job. SCOTT SCHALK: For taking the brunt of my neurosis and always cheering me on as if I were a brother. ADAM SANDLER: For telling me I'm full of it, and making me a better writer. KAREN WOHLMUTH: For treating me as if I were Michael Crichton. VANESSA VOSS: For letting me accidentally call her Tiffany and supporting me with enthusiasm in this endeavor regardless. GINA NYMAN: For giving me a clear perspective when I get into a moral, literary, or grammatical dilemma. JEFF THISTED: For keeping it light and fun during all situations via Homer Simpson impressions. TIFFANY BORS: For weeding through tons of fan mail and picking the gems . . . and for letting me call her Vanessa. TRAVIS SCHARIO: For schlepping out into the lines to hear contestants' stories, for his knowledge of *Price* trivia, and his terrific graphics. DAVID SCHWARTZ: For sharing the voluminous pages of his encyclopedic game-show mind. RUDI SIMPSON: For letting me ransack the CBS archives. LISA STAHL and HOPE VINITSKY: For their outstanding spontaneous photography. DAVE HALLMARK: For his technical wizardry and helping me capture the great moments on tape. DAVE FISHER: For letting me use CBS studios as if they were my own private toy. And finally, to the late, great MARK GOODSON: For giving me the chance to be creative and bringing my joyous career alive.

Contents

# Foreword

In this meticulously researched book, Stan Blits describes *The Price Is Right* on stage, backstage, and in the office.

Even our "loyal friends and true," a select group of people of rare good taste who watch our show every day, will learn a thing or two about *The Price Is Right*.

I am the executive producer and I did.

—Bob Barker

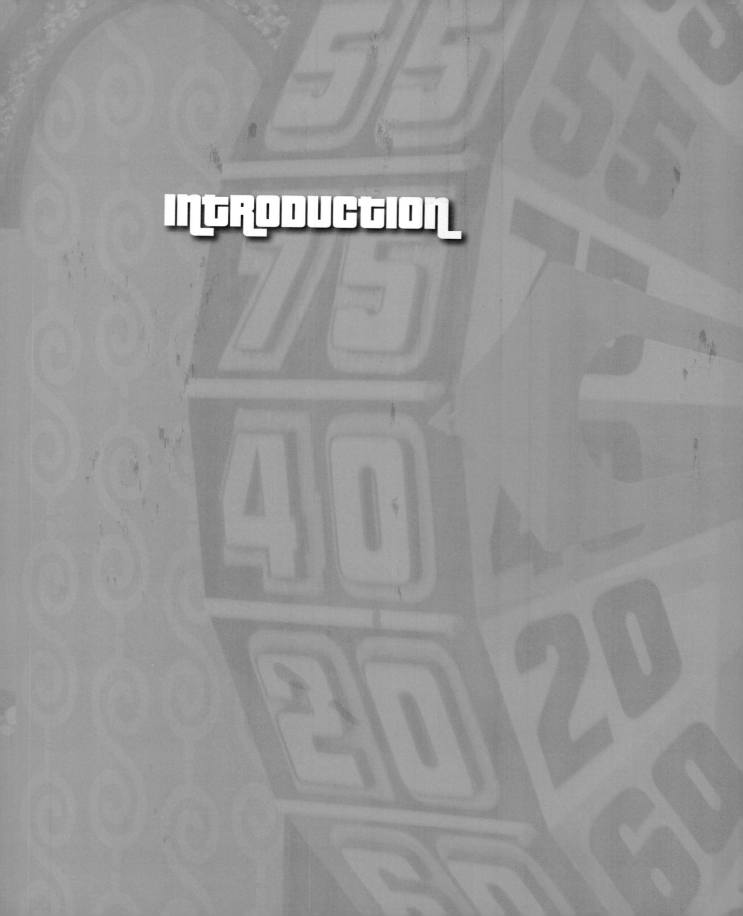

# INTRODUCTION

**WORKING IN THE TELEVISION INDUSTRY** gives you a perspective that almost nobody on earth gets to experience. That's one of the reasons I chose to go into show business. As I was riding in the backseat of my parents' car one day at the vulnerable yet rebellious age of twelve, we passed by the 20th Century Fox Studios. We could easily see through the gates and get a gander at the huge *Hello, Dolly!* street set in all its faux glory, right down to the plastic bougainvillea. I remember my father saying, "Now *there's* an interesting business. There's never a boring day." That moment stuck to me like cellophane to a finger on a high-static day. I tried to shake it off from time to time, but from that point on, I decided that showbiz was my destiny. I knew there wouldn't be a boring day, and I can honestly say, after twenty-eight years, there hasn't been.

I've had the good fortune of working on several hit game shows like *Now You See It, To Tell the Truth, Family Feud, Match Game,* and *Password,* as well as dozens of lesser-known shows. But most of my time has been spent on that iconic groundbreaking piece of pop culture that is known to just about everyone in the country. The show is *The Price Is Right,* that record-breaking institution of television that's been on the air for thirty-five years, and is still going strong, often topping the charts in the ratings.

For those of you who may have just crashed and fallen out of your Intergalactic Spiratron Stratocruisers and have not seen or heard of *The Price Is Right,* it's the one where they say "Come on down!" and hysterical people run out of the audience to play various games for prizes with legendary host Bob Barker.

I have three wonderfully creative jobs on the show. I'm the music director, which involves scouting, editing, and placing about forty pieces of music into the show while we tape.

I know what you're all thinking: "There's no music on that show . . . isn't it all just one piece played over and over again?" I've heard that a million times, and have gotten to the point where I can't blame anyone for saying it, as most people aren't aware of a lot of the elements that go into the making of a TV show. Without getting into a lecture on TV scoring, I'll just say that if you listen to the show with your back toward the television, you'll realize that *everything* in television and film is scored with background music specifically added for mood or theme.

My second job on the show is as a writer. I know what you're all thinking: "There's no writing on that show . . . isn't it all just impromptu screaming and yelling?" I've heard that about *two* million times, and, well, turn your back to the screen again and see above.

More specifically, there are showcase sketches at the end of the show that have themes. A few times a week, we'll do knockoffs of movies or TV shows like *Raiders of the Lost Ark, King Kong, The Twilight Zone*, or perhaps re-create Amelia Earhart's plane crash on a deserted island. We'll incorporate prizes into the sketch and have a little laugh as well. (See what those of you who haven't been watching have been missing?) Okay, it's not Shakespeare, but nevertheless it needs to be written by *someone* and I, along with a writing partner, spend hours each week creating these concepts.

Finally, and most amusingly, I'm the contestant coordinator. I interview and pick the contestants who "come on down" for the show. Again, I know what you're thinking: "There's no coordinating on that show . . . Don't they just pick names out of a hat?" Hey! Now I'm just going to slap you all.

It would be abundantly clear to you if you spent a little time with me during my interviews that some of the people who show up for game shows would not necessarily be awesome contestants. Great audience members, yes. Great rooters-on, definitely. Terrific devoted fans, no question, and we love them for it. Without them, we'd have no show. But some people are too scared or withdrawn to appear on a TV show. Sorry, folks, but just like the people who try out for other shows like *American Idol* (which our company produces) or shows like *So You Think You Can Dance*, it's painfully obvious that not everyone can sing, not everyone can dance, and not everyone looks like they're having fun on a game show. If we drew names out of a hat, we'd be off the air in a month . . . okay, maybe twenty-six weeks, but you'd be bored in a month.

It's casting of sorts. The "business of show" loves interesting people, whether they be actors, news stories, or game-show contestants. You've got to have some glitz and colorful characters to hold an audience, and *The Price Is Right* is certainly no exception.

I, along with my notetaker, go outside on that audience line at CBS Television City every day and interview about seventeen hundred people a week. That's right . . . you heard me. One thousand seven hundred crazy, excitable, dull, fascinating, mellow, out of control, disinterested, fanatic, hyper, sassy people . . . one at a time. Once again I know what you're thinking: "Yuck, get the antibacterial wipes!" (Maybe you're not thinking that, but it *has* occurred to me, and I'm sure by now I've developed immunity to every major airborne communicable disease in the western hemisphere.)

It's actually a lot of fun, and I've developed a quick technique for spotting the fun ones in the midst of what often appears more like a cheerleading session/standup comedy routine than an interview. When it comes to finding great contestants, sometimes it's a no-brainer. Sometimes I totally miss the boat. Other times I can intuitively spot a diamond in the rough, and if I play my cards right, I get to watch them shine onstage right before my eyes.

It's all just a testament to the unpredictability of people.

In the process of meeting these many people, it got me thinking about how amazingly diverse the planet is. Everyone's got a story, and believe me, they're dying to tell it, as evidenced by some of my outrageous interviews. It also made me wonder what these people's lives were like after they had the staggering experience of appearing on television and, better yet, coming home with a new ninety-thousand-dollar sports car. You'll meet Cousin Peggy, Aunt Jolene, Farmer Bill, the Butcher, the Baker, the Toilet Paper Maker . . . people from every walk of life. You'll learn about what got them to Hollywood to begin with, and you'll get my impression of them during the interview, how they performed on the show, and what became of them afterward, as well as the reaction of their family and friends.

You'll also get lots of insight into the backstage workings of this complex show. What goes on behind those big doors is staggering. Most people who visit the show are amazed by how much happens and how quickly and efficiently it comes together. It even makes *my* head spin, and I've been there for twenty-eight years!

*The Price Is Right* and its contestants are a microcosm of the American experience, and now you'll see what it's like as we witness what happens before, during, and after someone hears "Come on down!"

# 1

# CREATING AN EPIC SHOW
## How It's Done

**It was the dawn of mankind.** Earth's crust had just begun to harden as the magma from deep below the planet's surface oozed its way to the tumultuous world above and saw its first light of day. God reached down, and in his infinite wisdom, with the realization that terra firma alone wasn't enough to sustain life, He created *The Price Is Right.* Okay, maybe the show hasn't been on the air that long. But it *is* the longest running network game show in television history, and as far as many Americans are concerned, essential to life itself. Few people can remember a world without it, especially if you're under the age of forty.

Certainly 1972 wasn't the beginning of the planet, but the inception of *The Price Is Right* did eventually shake up the country a bit and did breathe some new life into the world. The show was about to become an important part of pop-culture history, and its debut came quickly, without much of the pomp and circumstance that would normally be expected of iconic media creations. Not even a pilot episode was shot for *The New Price Is Right,* as it was called then. It debuted the same day as two other new shows, *Joker's Wild* and *Gambit.* The show had been done in the fifties and early sixties with host Bill Cullen,

*When the show expanded to an hour, the big wheel was introduced to determine the two contestants for the showcase.*

but it was of a sedate nature. It had an almost intellectually dignified quality that so many shows of that day had. But times they were a-changin', and by the early seventies, a different breed of game show was in the works, with the same name, but certainly not the same style.

Taking a look at *The Price Is Right* today, the show seems to have been frozen in time. One can see its origins by the simplicity of some of its games and set design. No one seems to have wanted it to change much for fear of wrecking a good thing, and change it hasn't. It started out as a thirty-minute show with no big wheel, but in 1975 expanded to an hour.

New elements and colors as well as more complicated electronics in some of the games have updated it slightly, but all in all, it's a living, breathing time capsule. *The Price Is Right* is comfort food for the mind. People have had tantrums, like a child having been denied his blanket, when we've been preempted or missed a taping. When discussions of updating the show have arisen, there's always a resounding protest by all of us, as well as the viewers. Trying to modernize and "sophisticate" this show would be like putting béarnaise sauce on your Tater Tots. Thanks, but no thanks.

It did not enter the television medium with conformity. True, there had been other shows that bounded onto the television screen with bells, whistles, and screaming contestants. But this show was about to do many things that hadn't been done before.

First and foremost, the producers at that time, Mark Goodson and Bill Todman, had chosen a host who was perfect for the vision to which this show aspired. Goodson-Todman Productions had cranked out a multitude of megahits over the past decades and knew how to create a great show. Bill Todman took more of a backseat in the partnership as the businessman who handled the cash, and Mark Goodson was the hands-on creative guy. The ingenious Goodson, along with a team of producers, recruited the renowned host Bob Barker, who had a rich history of working with contestants on his then hit show *Truth or Consequences.* For a show that required impromptu interaction with contestants and knowledge of a complex television production, Bob was the perfect choice.

*Mark Goodson was considered the genius of game shows, and always had at least one show, if not several, on the air every single weekday for decades.*

He had panache, a great sense of humor, and knew how to get the most out of people in any given situation. He extracted comical moments from everyday folks and knew how to make stars of them with what seemed to be minimal effort. Don't let that fool you. It's not as easy as it looks. That's why he's so good at what he does, and why he has won more Emmys than any performer on television.

One of the unique features of the show is that different games are played each day. Why is this unique? Because it dared to go where no other shows would go, and that is to essentially change its content from day to day. How bold was it to create a variety of somewhat complex games and still make them simple enough for anyone to play whether they had seen them or not? The design of *The Price Is Right* games are quite impressive in that they need to be understood quickly with a relatively brief explanation by Bob. Remember, we've only got a limited amount of time, so if you create a game that's too complicated to understand with one explanation, the viewer will tune out. Of course, there have been exceptions, and this is one of the points that makes Bob Barker brilliant. A good example is a game we play called "Check Game." It's pretty simple, but from the very first time we played it, some contestants had a glazed-over look on their faces the minute they were asked by Bob, "Do you understand how to play, Josephine?" By the looks of it, you'd think the contestant was just asked to plot out a logarithmic chart for nuclear fusion. What does Bob do? He makes a totally amusing bit out of it by having some fun with the contestant. "Why does no one ever understand this game?" he'd declare. On the other side of that coin, if someone *did* understand the game, Bob would act either dumbfounded, or praise the contestant with glee as if they'd just come home from school with an A on their report card. Either way, it always gets a laugh . . . always. And that, my friends, is what makes an astonishingly great M.C.

*Bob instructs one of the very first winners of a showcase.*

Incorporating prices into a game is also not as easy as it seems. Yes, there are those simple "multiple choice" type of games. But the truly amusing ones utilize themes, like "Cliff Hangers," which uses the steps of a mountain climber to pace out a win, or trying to spell the word *car* in the game "Spelling Bee" by increasing your chances of pulling letters after successfully pricing small items.

Another subtle element that the show pioneered was a slicker soundtrack than had been heard before in this sort of setting. *The Price Is Right* was essentially the first game show to use a truly full orchestral jazz/pop/rock soundtrack, which gave it an intensity most people are unaware of.

Naturally people are always the lifeblood of a show like this. Audience members being called out of a crowd gave this format a wonderful drama that was undeniably exciting. You never knew what someone was going to do at any given moment. The contestants were given an opportunity to show their true selves, unrehearsed, uncoached, and unbridled. Even though interesting characters had appeared on other shows, Bob would allow some great personal background to sneak into their appearances by encouraging a mere comment or mischievous aspect of their personality. A little old lady would whisper in his ear, followed by Bob saying, "I'll meet you in the parking lot, Bessie." Acrobats would do Olympic-style flips on stage upon request. Opera singers would do fifteen-second arias.

Of course, I can't talk about *The Price Is Right* without talking about the nonhuman star of the show, namely prizes. It became clear that they had to do something to catch everyone's attention, and interestingly enough, Mark Goodson was not optimistic about the show at first because it was so heavily dependent on sponsor plugs and prize copy. He felt the audience would lose its patience with endless prize descriptions. Was this not a one-hour commercial disguised as a game show? It may have appeared that way on paper, but the various creative minds that developed the show felt it was so entertaining and so filled with variety that the audience would not get bored easily. How right they were.

By changing each and every show in its design, and adding fabulous showcases with prizes that would both wow and appall, you'd have pure entertainment. Yes, I said appall. C'mon, we've all seen stuff on the show we wouldn't wish on our worst enemy (would you really want to win a heart-shaped bed or a sofa shaped like lips?) . . . and yet it's still entertaining to see. Even a bad prize is worth talking about, and admit it, if all we gave away were refrigerators and dinettes, you'd be running for the remote faster than a duck headed for a June bug.

And strangely enough, no matter how little a contestant may appear to care for a prize at first, the second they know they've won, they jump for joy merely because they

*Giving cars away was always an exciting event, and in those days, the price had only four numbers!*

won. Have you ever won something at a picnic or company party and felt the elation of having your name or number called to come up front and pick up your new Thingamajig Inc. imprinted tote bag? Admit it. You needed it like a fish needs scuba gear, and yet you bounded back to your seat happy as a clam, head held high as you showed off to your fellow tablemates. And what's worse is that your tablemates didn't need one either, but were thinking, *Damn that Harry . . . I wish I'd have won that.*

Of course, the grand superstar of the prize world on this show is none other than "A new car!" That catchphrase has been uttered by various people in this country almost as many times as "Come on down!" and "Would you like fries with that?" Everyone who comes to the show wants to win one, and everyone watching at home loves to watch someone win one. *The Price Is Right* has given away more cars than any other show, and that's another ingredient in the formula that makes the show so exciting and makes people just *die* to "Come on down!"

And by the way, many people may not know this, but the first shows didn't summon each contestant to "Come on down!" right from the top. It was originally far more low-key as announcer Johnny Olson said, "Mary Smith, please stand up!" Mary would stand up, and then the second name would be called, "Joe Schmoe, please stand up!" The first four contestants would stand up this way, and then the announcer would tell them all to "Come on down" at the same time. Shortly after, it was decided that having the contestants just stand in place in the middle of the audience was a bit dull, so "Stand up" was given the ax and "Come on down" took over.

So how do you put on a TV show like *The Price Is Right* day after day? Do we just show up at work one day and, like Mickey Rooney and Judy Garland, say, "Hey! Let's put on a show! I'll get a barn, you make the costumes!" I don't think so. It takes a lot of hard work and know-how. So as I explain this to you, please, a word of caution: Do not attempt this at home. Doing your own TV show can be fatal, both financially and artistically.

## Start the Presses

Every week there is most likely a surge in the stock price for paper manufacturers due to the documents and graphics generated for this show. But who in this long line of administration starts the spinning of the pulp mill? On one level, it starts with the producer creating a sheet that outlines what games are going to be played. The show's producer, Roger Dobkowitz, plans this part in a way that actually has some strategy to it. Taking into consideration the budget, and how often we play each game, as well as one game's compatibility with another, he tries to get as much variety as possible with the more than seventy games that we have in stock. From day to day some games are more difficult than others, like in any other game show. After all, it should be entertaining, and you wouldn't want everyone walking off with absolutely *everything* every single day on every single show.

## A Plan of Attack

Then our associate producer, Kathy Greco (also known as "Fingers" on the air), goes into a room called the "war room" (a military term actually, not one we came up with). It's called that because it's the headquarters of planning a show's structure and prize content. It's sort of like planning a war, but with more tasteful accoutrements than one might find in a chief military officer's workplace, and with fewer deadly consequences (except for the upholstery found on some of our prize sofas . . . that's just decorator suicide). This war room has padded walls, and not only as a commentary on the emotional

*In the war room, dozens of trees are sacrificed for the hundreds of index cards used to plan the thousands of shows that please millions of people.*

well-being of our staff, but mainly because pins need to be stuck into it like a bulletin board.

Kathy sits at a long conference table across from this padded wall along with production coordinator Gina Nyman, who keeps track of any goof-ups or redundancies, and both have an overview of an entire week's worth of shows in one glance. Kathy goes into a computer database and assigns prizes to all the games and "One Bids" (a slick term for the prizes they bid on in contestant's row). She chooses what goes where, and there's a method to this madness too. A One Bid needs to be paired according to the game that follows it. For instance, you can't put a sailboat in a One Bid if the game right after it takes up so much space that there's no room for both of them on the stage, or one might block the other at some point. Another consideration is that prize scheduling directly involves plugging numbers into the games in various ways that affect the whole playing of the game, so she sort of has to back into some of the planning. Sometimes the tail wags the dog, sometimes the baby gets thrown out with the bathwater, sometimes one can paint one's self into a corner, but most important, I need to curb my idiomatic metaphors when describing show planning.

After all this brain-strain is worked out, a prize is written on a small index card along with a bunch of administrative information like retail price, our actual cost, and various reference numbers. The cards are then pinned onto the wall. By the time it's all done, the place looks messier than a frat house at spring break. At this point the room becomes a vitally important domain, top secret and secured by a multitude of bouncers, vigilantes, and armed killers. Anyone unauthorized entering the inner sanctum is shot immediately . . . shot a dirty look, that is. Okay, maybe not even that, but the office manager, Tiffany, has some really sharp pens, so don't mess with her.

## Script Trip

Following the planning phase, production coordinator Scott Schalk goes in and types the entire week's shows onto a form that becomes the foundation, if you will, on which everyone builds their subsequent work. This document makes a long journey through many people's eager little hands as the days progress. The script coordinator, Vanessa Voss, who pulls together and "builds" all the scripts, will assemble information about all the small grocery items and prizes and incorporate them into script form. Yes, Madge, there actually is a script for *The Price Is Right.* No, it's not like a movie or soap opera script. There's nothing in it about illegitimate births, torrid affairs, or life-altering medical procedures.

It's actually about thirty pages long and has all the prize copy in it that is to be read by the announcer. Vanessa also comes up with those fabulous lead lines you hear before each prize, like "It's a handy set of tools," or "It's an elegant new bracelet." The adjectives needed for an average show would give even Merriam-Webster a headache. I've actually seen a thesaurus burst into flames on Vanessa's desk after a long day's work.

The script also has details on the opening and closing of the show, including the big wheel, closed captioning plugs, showcases, and anything else that needs to be announced. Of course, Bob and the contestants are never scripted. All that is as real and spontaneous as it gets.

## Prized Possessions

And speaking of prizes and copy, oh what a tangled web *that* can be. In the old days, sponsors were more than happy to supply prizes for free, or at least for a substantial discount, in exchange for a credit on the show, but things have gotten so expensive now that those deals are not as easy to get. Even cars and trips are supplied at only a slight discount to us, so we do get a better deal on stuff than you would if you, Joe Consumer, just headed down to your local Prizes-R-Us store at the mall, but it ain't a free-for-all or bargain-basement time like everyone thinks.

CBS has an entire department called Promotional Placement and Awards that dedicates its time to, among many other things, finding deals on prizes. Manufacturers have strict guidelines on how their products must be shown, so there are endless records cataloged in computers (they used to be on volumes of paper in notebooks before computers existed . . . that's how long this show has been on the air!). Something called a P.I., or prize information form, indicates the frequency of appearance of their product, along with the exact wording of how they want their product described. Many manufacturers don't want to overexpose their product, or only make deals for a limited amount of showings, so that must all be kept track of. One obsessive representative of a famous brand of washer/dryer was adamant about not opening the lid of their washers while on camera. They felt it wasn't attractive. Thank God, because we wouldn't want an ugly appliance on TV now, would we?

When the prize deals are made, the wholesalers and retailers send over the loot and it's hauled into the CBS warehouse. There a staff of people check them out, make records of them, and shuffle them into a very special place for safekeeping. And what a place it is! This prize dungeon is underneath CBS TV City and encompasses acres of space. In addition there are parking lots filled to the brim with cars, boats, trailers, Jet Skis, and just about anything else you can dream up that would be a prize. It's like Costco on steroids. And speaking of meds, the small items like aspirin bottles, arthritis medicine, cookies, and cans of creamed corn are all kept down there too. So listen up, all you survivalists! If there's ever a nuclear holocaust, head for the bowels of CBS and you'll be able to live for years, in addition to having a fabulous recliner to sit on in which to contemplate the rest of eternity with that extra irradiated arm you grew.

## The World's a Stage

While all this scripting is going on, production coordinator Karen Wohlmuth is working with the director, Bart Eskander, on staging the show. She's got a staging sheet with a layout of the entire stage, a kind of blueprint from above. With prizes and set pieces as a guide, she and the director need to make sure there are no collisions, contradictions, or bottlenecks in the movement and placement of things. Copies of the staging sheets are distributed to all the stagehands too so that everyone can get an overview of the show. It all fits together like a big complicated puzzle. The gears in this well-oiled clock are carefully carved out ahead of time, cog interlocking with cog, so that each moment meshes beautifully, with no snags . . . uh, at least that's the intention. Sometimes it just doesn't work that way, but overall, it actually goes amazingly well, and to this day, I'm still truly amazed that it all gets done as smoothly as it does.

After the producer has selected the cars to appear on the show, one of our production staff members, Jeff Thisted, deals with the administration that is required for cars. He then prepares a form called a routine sheet, which contains all the prices of every prize on it. (Boy, wouldn't you like to get your hands on *that* one?) It will later be used by everyone during the taping to monitor wins and losses. Jeff is also what I call the show's cheerleader. He stands at the edge of the stage and encourages everyone in the audience to applaud when it's needed, especially after the last contestant has come on down and the horrific reality has set into every brain in that studio that no more people will be called down to win anything.

Also being generated by Gina at this point are graphic orders for the tons of printed matter that gets stuck up onto the actual games. She also creates a prop sheet filled with everything from wardrobe and special effects to set descriptions and unusual custom props.

After everything's been drawn up and distributed, Karen gives our cameramen shot sheets, which are sort of step-by-step instructions on what's going to come up for them. There are four cameras, and each camera has different notes—for instance one shot sheet could say:

1. Turntable, door 2, center stage
2. Audience sweep to Bob's bow
3. Close-up of grocery items, pan
4. Over roof of car—driver—zoom out
5. Over roof of car—passenger—tilt up, peekaboo of model through window—zoom out

And so forth.

Preparation of the shots is vital by the time we rehearse the show because the director will eventually call which camera he wants to shoot a particular action. By showtime whatever the director calls out gets zapped through hundreds of miles of cables and ultimately onto a videotape deep in the catacombs of CBS, where mad-scientist-like technicians with wild hair and wicked laughs make sure we actually have an image that stuck.

## Meet and Potatoes

By the time we have deforested a small continent, we're ready to have meetings with all the various factions of production.

The staging meeting consists of a group of key people who can work out every detail,

*Our staging meeting is where everyone agrees to agree . . . or not. All the details get ironed out here to make sure we're all on the same page.*

like a special effect, set pieces, or a wardrobe color. This is the speak-now-or-forever-hold-your-peace meeting. If we need a ten-foot pile of potatoes stacked in the bed of a truck, this is when we tell the set decorators how it should look. Clarity is of the essence. For instance, if we're doing a Noah's Ark showcase, and you tell the art director to build you a twenty-foot phony ship, but you really meant an *ark,* and you didn't say *ark* specifically, by the time the show rolls around in a couple of weeks, Noah is going to look pretty stupid if a pirate ship shows up. Communicate, people! Communicate!

## Melodic Mayhem

When I receive a script and a show rundown, I'll go over it and start to score the show with music. Scoring, in this case, is laying in prerecorded music for which I've scouted with various composers over the years and edited with my handy-dandy computerized editor. Everything is supported with music on the show: wins, losses, diamond rings, cars, sofas, the whole enchilada (yes, we actually gave away enchiladas and burritos on the show once). Of course, the most recognizable piece is the main theme, which we use to open and close the show, as well as go to every commercial. This hasn't changed in thirty-five years, but for the most part has been pretty much taken for granted by the average viewer. I can tell you, though, that it has become painfully clear how important music is to the feel of the show when I've had a technical problem and *nothing* played during the showing of, let's say, a car. The silence is deafening.

Not only that, but improving a character or sketch with a piece of music is very important in any show you're doing. If you're going to do a showcase sketch knocking off Indiana Jones, you'd better have a piece of music that knocks off that sound too, or your sketch turns dull and lifeless.

## Affected Effective Effects

Mark Goodson pioneered the sound effects that everyone seems to be familiar with in game shows. Some of our games have been designed so that there isn't a clear visual indication that there's a win or a loss. (Nothing actually flips down or lights up to reveal a right price.) How does Bob know if a contestant is a winner or loser? It often depends entirely on a bell, a buzzer, or a variety of other interesting sounds. If there's an overbid in contestant's row, a buzz tells Bob, who then tells the contestants. In a game called "Bonkers," the contestant runs frantically to place disks in the proper location on a large game board and runs back to hit a button followed by nothing other than a bell or a buzzer. As a matter of fact, *The Price Is Right* has taken it to a whole new level. Some sound effects are created specifically from scratch for certain games. A game called "One Away" uses a car horn to tell people whether an answer is right. Bob has made a whole routine out of it, as he always does so well.

He tells the contestant to ask the sound-effects person, "Ladies, do I have one number right?" which, if correct, would be followed by a car *HOOOOONK!* He'll continue by prompting the contestant to ask again. "Ladies, do I have two numbers right?" ... *HOOOOOONK!* Interesting thing here is that if there's *no* honk, the audience moans because that means there are no more numbers correct. Silence has essentially become the sound effect in this case.

We'll often have meetings on just sound effects. I've sat with a sound engineer named Hope Vinitsky for hours on end playing through various synthesized zips, zonks, chimes, and kabloowees, and sometimes combined and played all at once in order to come up with a perfect and unique sound. In film there is something called a Foley artist. This is a person who drops a wet sandbag on the floor, records it, and uses it as the sound of a dead body dropping to the ground for a movie. We've done a lot of our own Foley work for *Price* showcases, where the sound-effects person dribbles gravel onto glass to make it sound like rain on a window, or sticks a microphone in a hairdryer to make the sound of a hurricane. It's a really fun and bizarre way to make a living, but then again, everything in a TV studio is bizarre compared to the real world.

## Art for Our Sake

As all those elements are put into place, various graphics are also being created for all the games based on the order that was submitted earlier. Everything from printing numbers on cardboard to graphics with grocery item names on them are designed, drawn, or printed right there in the art and graphics department at CBS. A team of talented artists get long lists for upcoming shows, and subsequently send down stacks of new graphics every week. The graphics that are used eventually get filed away after every show in rows and rows of huge cabinets backstage. Because we've been on the air so long, the backstage wings of studio 33 look like the Smithsonian archives. It does save loads of money, though, and remember, it is a business, so wherever they can save cash, they do. The cost of some of these works of art would make some people's hair stand on end. Network artists are not cheap, and I've known some art cards to cost as much as a nice piece of gallery art. And the tragic thing is that after some of them are used, if they get a smudge or little rip in them, they get tossed. Picasso would roll over in his grave.

## Curbing the Cash Cow

Are you all getting the idea of why television shows cost so much to produce? Just ask our executive in charge of production, Sue MacIntyre. She's what we call a "Digit Dick." (You know, like Dick Tracy, the detective.) That's exactly what she does. She hunts down overspenders like a wolf in the night. She works out budgets. She negotiates crews. She leaps tall network executives in a single bound. She, along with executive consultant Syd Vinnedge, actually keeps track of all the numbers, contracts, and costs of running the show. On any given day, one can see her hunched over her computer like a turn-of-the-century banker on a ciphering device.

*"The Aviator" was a very cute and expensive showcase inspired by the feature film of the same name, but with a* Price Is Right *twist.*

I've had my virtual hand slapped a time or two by her. Yeah, I've gotten a bit carried away with a showcase concept. C'mon, is it really too much to ask for a 747 to land in the studio followed by an explosion of gold dust with dancing elves flying out of an alien spaceship via laser transporter beam? Big deal. I was in a good mood the day I thought of it. I didn't get the 747 or the elves, but I did get a cute cartoonish biplane with a turning propeller, clouds, and a wind machine for my "Aviator" showcase. Good enough.

*The Price Is Right* is, in some respects, an expensive show to produce, as compared to, let's say, a talk show. In other ways, it's really not that expensive at all when you think about a prime-time comedy or drama. Everyone knows the eight-digit salaries doled out to actors and their productions in prime time. But daytime has a smaller and more limited audience, so the advertisers don't pay as much to put their product on the air as nighttime advertisers do. The budgets have gotten tighter and tighter over the years as advertisers are wary of spending zillions to put a product on a morning game show or soap opera. Cable has stolen much of the staple audience we used to have over the years, and with that mass departure went the bucks we make.

But don't cry for us, Argentina. We're fine. It's still a good business and we try not to be too big a crybaby over the good ol' days of fat profits and endless showers of cash from Proctor and Gamble. The game has changed, but the motivation hasn't. When you've got a high-profile iconic blockbuster household-name show attached to your company's roster, you could have worse things to complain about.

# 2

# THE WAY WE WERE

## The Early Years
## of the Show

**IF you've watched any** of your favorite TV shows for years and then later watched a rerun, you probably remember thinking *Holy moly! This show really changed,* even though it didn't actually change in structure. Everyone's younger, the set looks somewhat different, and everything looks a little strange.

Since such a vast amount of time has passed since the first *Price Is Right* aired, it is particularly jolting to watch the first shows. Everyone in the audience was dressed a bit more conservatively. No flip-flops, torn jeans, or swim trunks were seen on TV game shows in 1972. No wildly painted T-shirts on *The Price Is Right* yet either. As a matter of fact, probably not many T-shirts were worn at all because the collared shirt was pretty much the standard male wardrobe. Being on TV seemed to be a bigger deal back then somehow, as there was no reality programming and the informal format that you see nowadays in many shows was totally unfamiliar. Shows such as *Big Brother* and the like have gotten people used to watching folks running around in their skivvies.

Not only were the people an indicator of the time, but the set had a sort of earth-tone typical seventies look about it that almost made it sepia-like due to the lower resolution TV cameras of that day. In comparison with the high-definition digital equipment we use today, it was more akin to looking at a Polaroid print than a sharp digital picture.

There was more piñata-colored stucco on that set

*Notice how the dress code was different. A suit and tie was not that uncommon for a contestant.*

than a Tijuana taco joint. And of course something that was a typical symbol of the day that still remains in one form or another is the daisy, a throwback to the hippie flower child days of the sixties and early seventies.

*The color TV set was a staple prize of the game-show world, and in those days most households were still watching the show in black and white.*

The set was designed by a man named Don Roberts, who also designed the set for the hit show *All in the Family.*

Bob had dark hair with long sideburns and wore suits typical of that period. Contestants were doing things that hadn't really been seen much before on other shows, like beating up the host. It made for some really funny television, and many a montage has been assembled of Bob getting clobbered, lifted off the floor, and chased around the stage. Audience members just can't resist the temptation to attack Bob, and now, as a very funny bit, Bob summons a Barker Beauty to stand between him and the crazed contestant for protection, or he'll just run behind a game.

There are some astonishing differences in content if you watch the older shows. If you were able to see some of the original gags we pulled off in the early days, you'd also be painfully aware of what's changed in our society, particularly the political correctness that has come to the forefront of just about everything.

We did a showcase called "Star Bores" back in the seventies. Since everything from the original *Star Wars* was parodied, it was vital to get a good hook into the sketch like the famous line from the movie, "May the force be with you." The producers then decided to use the phrase "May the sauce be with you," making Luke Skywalker a raging alcoholic and referring of course to a bottle of booze. Not only that, they had announcer Johnny Olson as Luke sitting in the prize car at the end of the showcase, drinking out of a bottle in a paper bag. Wow, I think I just heard a couple of lawyers bound out of their leather chairs.

Another character we did was a homeless person. In those days we called them hoboes, but there was no mistaking that this chick was a homeless bag lady. She staggered drunk through the set and actually stuck her head in the prize oven while on her knees. Did I just hear a blood vessel burst at the Anti-Defamation League?

Bob has had an indelible influence on the content of the show. In the early years, the fur coat was a staple of the game-show prize giveaway. It represented glamour, every woman wanted one, and it was the kind of status symbol that essentially doesn't exist today in the world of prizes. Bob became a staunch animal rights activist over the years, and so we eliminated any furs on the show. Anything related to animal cruelty was rightfully gotten rid of and we never show any animal products even in the form of props . . . only plastic veggies on a grill or in a fridge. (Bob is a strict vegan.) We stopped giving away aquariums, and certainly wouldn't be touting the benefits of fishing equipment on a show that rallies to the cause of animal rights.

The earliest shows featured cars of all kinds, from Mazdas to Jaguars. We felt strongly about supporting the American economy, so we started to give away only American brand cars. For a while, we weren't even giving away any General Motors cars because many years ago it was discovered that General Motors used live animals in crash tests (a practice that has since stopped). This was totally unacceptable to many viewers, and certainly to Bob, so there were many years of shows in which you wouldn't see a Cadillac or Chevy.

*One of the first Barker Beauties, Janice Pennnington, models a Chevy.*

Believe it or not, television had a sort of backlash of conservatism in the eighties. With the "family values" political atmosphere surfacing, we started to tone down some of the more risqué elements of the show. As a result, we stopped putting models in bikinis and put them in more conservative one-piece swim suits, and to this day, that is still the case. There was a game called "Bump," which had a model swaying and grinding her hips and hitting a series of numbers, essentially "bumping" the correct price in place. It definitely had a sexual overtone. It was around for a little while, but also went the way of the abovementioned drunk, seminaked, suicidal, vagrant characters, never to be seen again.

April Fools' was always a fun day to pull off some pranks both on and off the air. Especially messing with the contestant. We stopped doing it after many years because it became so predictable that people were expecting it, and there's nothing more disappointing than a blah response from someone after you've spent all this time and money preparing a practical joke.

One of the things we would do was have a totally fictitious showcase in which we'd show cruddy prizes. A chandelier would fly in, but instead of stopping, it would continue to fly in and crash right through the dining room table below it, destroying the table. Next we'd offer a trip to Flushing, New York. (No offense to you guys in Flushing, but you all know as well as I that you're not a world tourist destination.) At the end of the showcase, we'd roll on a really old beat-up car. The contestant would look totally baffled after Bob would ask them what they wanted to bid. After adequate torture time had lapsed, Bob would say, "April fools!" and we'd open the door to a fabulously expensive Cadillac on which they would bid. We were soooo mean.

It was all in good fun of course, and the world accepted what we did with open minds because that was the mentality of the day. As the politics of this nation changed, we became aware of our content whether we liked it or not. One of the first complaints I remember hearing about was because of a showcase in which we were tossing hot dogs over a fence. A woman wrote that, with all the hunger in the world, why on earth would we waste food like that? It may have been a stretch, but suddenly it set in that the country had become sensitive to almost everything, and so we paid attention and watched our Ps and Qs a bit more closely.

# 3

# FROM MOVING MOUNTAINS TO MASCARA

## A Typical Day on the Set

## Every Day Is Moving Day

It starts a lot earlier than most businesses do. The setup of *The Price Is Right* involves an unimaginable amount of time, people, and elements. Starbucks and alarm clocks are the tools of survival in this town. Long before anyone shows up to scream and shout in the audience at studio 33 of CBS Television City, there are sleepy-headed scenic designers, set decorators, prop folks, and grips making it all pretty for you. After all, Barker's Beauties and refrigerators need a little help to look their best, and when you see one of those gorgeous things on camera (the fridges, not the beauties) you're going to want to see some fake milk and lettuce in there rather than just an empty metal box. You're also going to want to see paintings on the walls in the bedrooms, flowers on the tables, plants around the playhouse, and beautifully fanned silverware on a red felt disk.

For those of you who have experienced the horrors of moving, and who among us hasn't, imagine having to do that every day, and then at the end of the day, having to pack it all up again. Set decorator Richard Domabyl and his crew painstakingly tend to all this at ungodly hours. Take a look at the average decorating crew on a Thursday, and their bloodshot eyes and *don't-talk-to-me-or-I'll-kill-you* demeanor will say it all. I've shown up to the set at nine A.M. and seen crew members sound asleep on prize sofas, draped face-down over motorcycle handlebars like dead accident victims, and curled up in a corner hugging a case of antacids. It's a lot of exhausting work, possibly even thankless, as most viewers are unaware that someone actually does this job. Remember, folks, those drapes don't hang themselves, although after a week of taping, some set decorators do.

## It's Not Easy Being Green

As everyone slowly trickles into the studio at various hours, you can see one of the first meetings happening in what is known as the greenroom, a generic word in show business that goes way back and describes any room in a studio that is a waiting room/meeting room for talent and staff. You'll hear it referred to on shows like *Letterman*, or any other talk show for that matter. Our greenroom has been used to death. From party central, to dressing room, to locker room, to crew's napping quarters, it's the most used/abused space in the place. The meeting we're seeing at this early hour is headed by the show's director, Bart Eskander, and includes Rich Fields, the announcer, and all the models. They take this time to go over various details of their performance, placement on the stage, and any prize fondling directions they may need to be primed on. In addition, the showcase sketches are described to them, and if the models are playing any characters, they will have a chat about what those characters are and how they'll look and act (it's not easy playing a mermaid with bound legs or a gypsy while on a game-show stage).

## Seeing the Light

While this is all happening, the lighting crew is making sure that Bob Barker will look good, as well as all the prizes, the audience, and anything else that you'd actually want to see without squinting. One of our staff members describes our show as looking like "it is shot on the sun." Yes, it's all awash in painfully bright light, but like everything else, it is not taken for granted if suddenly Bob steps onto a set and a big dark spot appears on his face, as if there were an eclipse onstage.

Lighting is often used for dramatic purposes as well. The soaps are known for this due to their intensely dramatic themes. There have been showcases where we've blacked out the stage to emulate a murder mystery, followed by a pretaped scream. Sometimes I'll ask for lightning and thunder when the script has a Philip Marlowe mystery plot in it and it starts with the cliché "It was a dark and stormy night." It's easy to overlook details like that, but a person actually sets and programs a dedicated light among the hundreds of other lights just for that purpose.

And by the way, if you're paranoid and have any fear of things falling on you, never enter a television studio. If you look up into the catwalks and scaffolding, you'll see an ocean of huge lights, television monitors, and rigging that would give you a chill. It looks like a bat cave, with zillions of things hanging and staring down at you. There are security chains holding up everything, but think about it. Would you go to bed at night with your jumbo TV precariously hanging over your head? No matter how many chains are holding that thing up, I doubt you would get a good night's sleep. I've gotten used to it, but occasionally, I look up and notice it and I'm amazed at how much weight is looming overhead. Each light can weigh hundreds of pounds. They're made of iron, glass, steel, and many other lethal gravity-loving materials.

There have been some ugly incidents involving lights. No, not an overlit acne scar on a model, but rather an occasional light has made its way down and clobbered a stagehand. This is usually followed by a nice bevy of workers' comp representatives and drooling attorneys spreading out their documents on tables like gingham cloths at a litigious picnic.

One time there was a lamp that popped during a show. It sounded like a gun going off, and suddenly searing hot cinders followed by a string of smoke made their way down to an audience member and burned a nice hole in the top of her scalp. I don't know if that led to any settlements, but I bet the woman wore a hat for a very long time.

## Sound Advice

Barring any searing flesh, at this time the audio crew is also setting up, testing every element of the show's sound. Here's another aspect of the show that's invisible. This is a communications business, but nothing gets communicated if you can't hear it, so just listen to the show sometime. There's a ton of audio coming from all directions, and it has to be nicely escorted to the videotape via the sound mixer, David Vaughn. Every single element needs to be "mixed," or balanced, including sound coming from Bob Barker, the four contestants, the announcer, the audience reaction, sound effects, music, and any enhancements to the soundtrack that is lacking naturally, which is known as "sweetening." All this is funneled up to the show's audio guy, who has a console the size of Long Island with enough knobs and buttons to make a jet fighter pilot nauseous.

## Being Pushy

If you look across the stage right about now, you'll hear the art director, Bente Christensen, shouting out directions to dozens of stagehands to "Move the motor home to the left, no right, no farther downstage. Okay, mark it!" At which point someone puts colored tape on the floor so that when the time comes, they can roll that prize right onto its mark with no question of where it goes. This makes the taping go quickly and quietly. Hours are spent shoving stuff around to get the perfect position for everything you can imagine. Okay, I'm about to wreck something for you. If you watch the show on the air, take a look at the floor. You may never have noticed it before, but it looks like a child has tossed confetti all over the stage. Tape marks of all colors spatter the stage, and it's quite messy. Your mother would be upset with a floor like this at home, but here it's all about efficiency.

Back in the depths of the CBS lot lurk the more than seventy games that we play on the show. They must be hauled out and prepared for a quick entry when they're needed. Some are so big they need jumbo-jet-style tuggers to push them down the hallway. Most can be pushed by a couple of grips (called that because they actually "grip" onto something to move it . . . that's their job, really!). Each and every game that is brought out is tested and tested again. Some of these games, even to my surprise, have amazingly complex electronics behind them. That's why some of them cost over thirty thousand dollars to build. They are run through a series of electronic tests because if they fail during a taping, it could not only disrupt the whole show, it would require an already antsy audience to wait for its repair, and we don't want to "kill" a great audience now, do we? The show is taped as if it is live. It's done in just a bit over an hour, and the commercial time is used to change sets . . . not a whole lot of time to move a Cadillac and a "Cliff Hangers" mountain.

## The Vanity Fair

As the models show up, it's fun to see how they look in sweats and no makeup. Amazing that they're still beautiful, but in an earthy I'm-hanging-around-the-house sort of way. At this point, the wardrobe, makeup, and hair folks are starting to set up shop. Special rooms have been designated for this, and it's fun to see the gadgets they've got to do all these extreme makeovers.

## Fashion Sense and Nonsense

The clothes that are worn during the show are brought out in the morning by our costume stylist, Robin Gurney. These outfits are supplied by various stores and designers in exchange for a screen credit at the end of the show.

The bizarre costumes that are worn by the models during the showcase sketches are often designed especially for the show if they can't be found "off the rack." Obviously when a model is playing the part of a pyramid, a mouse, or a chubby Danish smorgasbord hostess, you can't always go to your local costume shop or your eccentric Aunt Gertrude's attic.

Our designer has created some of the most innovative outfits I've ever seen. From dressing up a woman to look like an old bearded tailor named Shlomo to robots in high heels with wheels, the comedy is often in the details of the wardrobe. One of the prop storage boxes backstage has pictures stuck all over it of dozens of models donning hundreds of strange outfits. It looks like the bulletin board for a carnival freak show, but never ceases to get a laugh when people walk by.

## Wiggin' Out

Our hair stylist, Mira Wilder, has had her share of challenges too. Aside from the multitude of hair textures and style challenges she has to deal with on a daily basis as various women pass through her stylist chair, she also creates wigs that

*Models always seem to be getting ready for something at any given moment.*

*A model's hair is often redone multiple times in one day.*

astonish. We did a showcase about Rapunzel and needed to have a model stand in a tower while draping ten feet of hair down to retrieve prizes and pull them up in her hair. Several meetings were had to discuss how this was going to be done. Should it be red-dyed braided rope? Should it be yarn? We weren't sure what would look good on camera, and after much debate, it ended up being yards of artificial hair and it looked great.

We also did a showcase where the hairdos were emulating famous landmarks, like the Eiffel Tower and the Sydney Opera House. We went online

*Rapunzel's hair was something that required a lot of thought.*

to get as many photos of these historic structures as we could, and Mira used them to model the weirdest set of wigs you've ever seen. I could hear Cher's envious cry in the distance.

## Perfecting Perfection

I've watched a model having her makeup applied, and the tricks of the trade are dazzling. Eye size gets doubled, cheekbones get protruded, and lips get enhanced without the pain of silicone injections! And all with people-paint!

The makeup artist, Carol Wood, has a whole set of completely different challenges that vary from person to person. She's got more paint and brushes in that dressing room than Home Depot. Television can be an unforgiving medium, especially because a show like *The Price Is Right* is lit so brightly. You'd think that what you see is what you get, but if you've ever seen a flash picture of yourself that makes you want to bury your head in concrete for all eternity, you know what I mean. Every angle needs to look good, and depending on who your lighting

*Flawless makeup makes flawless models.*

director is and what the color of the set is, the makeup person has to readjust her work accordingly.

When Bob Barker went from dark hair to white hair, there was quite an adjustment period for his makeup to look good on camera. Sometimes the foundation was too dark, or too light, or seemed too yellow or too orange on camera, so several screen tests were done to make it as natural as possible. When our set was repainted in a predominantly blue tone, it made Bob look washed out, so we readjusted the set colors, as well as the makeup. It's not always as much about correcting flaws as it is about depth and contrast. Eyes, eyebrows, sideburns . . . they can all disappear on camera if not attended to by a makeup artist.

## Well, Isn't That Special?

The special effects and electric crew also checks out every electronic aspect of the show. Large custom-made consoles sit onstage with a crew operating them like game-show mission control. They also operate any movielike special effects such as explosive flash pots, fire, breakaway sets, bizarre mechanical props, buckets of water dumping on models, or anything else we can conjure up in a showcase to thoroughly distract you from your ironing and screaming kids in the morning.

## Flying High

While this is going on, doom is lurking overhead. Walls that "fly" in from the ceiling are hung from long steel tubes, brought down, and marked by a flyman. He's the guy who drops anything and everything, from baskets to trip walls. Even motor scooters have been known to pull a Peter Pan stunt now and then. If it's suspended and moving, it's the flyman who does it. A good flyman is smooth and seamless. A bad one can kill. He's got to mark all those heavy cables in places that tell him when to stop dropping five-hundred-pound props onto the stage. Occasionally he'll miss the mark, causing a crash onstage that sounds like a redwood falling onto a house. It scares the tar out of most of us, and following an "oops" from the flyguy comes a series of phone calls to the stage crew's life insurance agents.

## Practice Makes Perfect

After all the basic preparations for rehearsal have been made, another meeting is called in the greenroom about half an hour before we rehearse. This meeting requires the director, stage managers, assistant director, models, announcer, production coordinators, and lots of paper. Everyone has a staging sheet that lays out, in drawing form, the entire show for the day, sort of like a map of the stage and what will appear on it. The director goes through every detail of the show, in addition to assigning models to various areas onstage, and camera shooting patterns, which the director has marked in his own script.

While choreographing the models, it's important for them to do *exactly* the same moves on the show as they do in rehearsal, or they may find themselves gesturing their pretty little hands right over a manufacturer's logo, which would lead to a stop tape, which would lead to a reshoot, which would lead to thousands of dollars in overtime costs, which would lead to my not getting a Christmas bonus this year. Truly tragic.

## Hurry Up and Wait

Showbiz is known for having a lot of sitting around while waiting for other people to do stuff. Then, all of a sudden, someone shouts, "I need it now! Right now! What's taking so long?" If you're impatient, this is not the career for you. Rehearsals are a bit like that.

As soon as everyone has fulfilled his or her artistic or technical duties, it's time to practice what we've preached in meetings for the last few hours. The rehearsal is basically for everyone except Bob and the contestants, of course. It's the time when all the cameras practice their moves, the models practice theirs, and the announcer works through oodles of copy. Rehearsal is a bit discombobulating to the average visitor. In order to save time, the whole show is rehearsed out of sequence. The showcases come first so that their intricate contents can be moved off the stage and placed strategically in the halls for return at the end of the show taping. The rest of the stuff comes when it comes. Sometimes props are so buried behind other props that it just makes more sense to bring things on when they're available rather than shuffling everything around to fit the script. The wheel gets spun to make sure that the beeps are beeping and the electronic readouts are reading out, and games are carefully guided in one at a time like big, cumbersome animals at a fair.

Dozens of stagehands are divided up into various crews, or teams, and work various places. There's the stage crew and the hall crew. The hall crew gets games and prizes and shoves them toward the stage through a gigantic "elephant door" (probably so named because it's so large you could get an elephant through it), at which point the stage crew grabs them and places them on those famous tape marks that I talked about earlier. Then the models are put in place by one of our three stage managers, the director cues everyone to do their thing, and the announcer reads the script.

When it's all rehearsed, and everyone is confident that they can actually pull this whole thing off, a break is called for about an hour. Everyone scurries off to the commissary or to their cell phones for a moment of solitude before the big event.

# 4
# THE MODEL OF PERFECTION
## Barker's Beauties

**Being a model on a game show** is one of those enviable jobs that is perceived as glamorous, albeit predictable. You show up to work, you get all pretty, and you get lots of attention. People dote all over you with makeup, hairbrushes, beautiful glamorous dresses. You know the routine. But most women who audition to be a Barker Beauty have no idea what they're in for. They probably think the day is simply going to be filled with your standard refrigerator stroking, toothpaste handling, and diamond fondling. Yeah, there's a lot of that. But be warned, all you pretty things out there. It ain't always so pretty. We've blacked out more teeth and ratted more hair in creating showcase characters than a vaudevillian road show, and everyone who wants to be in this show's limelight has to put up with being uglified once in a while.

I remember having an amusing conversation with one of the original producers of the show, Jay Wolpert, about what he was looking for in a model back in the seventies. He was big

*Surely, doing a scene from* Frankenstein *is a rarity in the modeling world.*

on swashbuckling films . . . you know, the whole Errol Flynn genre with sword-fights and rope-swinging. He created a swashbuckling showcase in which various models would audition as pirates, sword and all. All the models seemed to be too shy to abandon themselves in the character. But when one model almost got "stabbed" in the groin area, she dropped her sword, quickly grabbed her crotch with both hands, and had a broad, painful expression on her face . . . kind of an oh-crap-that-hurts look.

She was instantly hired.

One of the models from day one was Janice Pennington. She was a classic beauty, and had been seen in the television comedy show *Rowan and Martin's Laugh-In* in the sixties as the girl dancing with body paint all over her. She had also done some *Playboy* layouts, and was a great choice as a model on the show. She had a great sense of humor, and could also pull off the comic characters that were needed. Anitra Ford joined her and later left to pursue an acting career.

There's much to learn and memorize in the body of the show as well. Because there are over seventy games, the models must know the routines for revealing prices. They have to know when cameras are on them, when to flip a card around, when to hit but-

tons or show a price behind a flap, and even how to work a cash register. Even though there are stage managers to help them get into position and prompt them if they need it, a good model who is on the ball will make the workings of the backstage all that much easier and smoother.

Every morning each model receives a staging sheet in a meeting, and while listening to the director and his staging instructions and assignments, they will diligently need to make notes with all directions of where to be and what to do.

Sometimes the requirements are tight and rigid. "Can you make it across the stage in fifteen seconds in order to show the motorcycle?" might be one of the questions asked. If the answer is yes, then come showtime, you'll often see a blur of a model dashing across the stage to hit her mark only milliseconds before that big door opens up. I've actually seen one slide into the door like a baseball player at home plate, get up, quickly compose herself, and gracefully pose when the camera cut to her. Then, as quickly as she came into the picture, she's out

*We think that Da Vinci would have approved of our model's version of his masterpiece.*

again, heading to wardrobe to change into a witch outfit or squeeze into a bathing suit. Hey ladies, try to run a marathon in five-inch spike heels sometime, and on shiny linoleum tile to boot. It's farcical and, frankly, watching these

*The "First Ladies" of* The Price Is Right: *Anitra Ford and Janice Pennington as Barker Beauties.*

girls, I'm glad I get to wear comfortable sport shoes and clothes when I go to work. It's a painful job, but someone's got to do it.

Many of these models have had no acting experience, and granted, we're not doing the death scene from *Romeo and Juliet* here, but it does take an abandonment of inhibition to appear natural, and to portray an idea in a sketch with facial expressions and movements. It also takes those qualities to be merely appealing when modeling *any* prize on the show. New models often seem a bit stiff in movement, and afraid to be themselves. The audience picks up on this, and the better they perform, the more the viewer falls in love with them. The director and stage managers have helped many an uptight model come out of her shell. Many of these women come from the print world, and are not familiar with sketch comedy or broad facial expressions at all. It's merely pose and snap, pose and snap. Then there are those models who are great at it and have had a bit of theater and TV background. They will often get cast into the more difficult showcase sketches that require a whole array of gestures and movements that completely make the

*Putting models in zany situations is a trademark of our showcases.*

sketch work. After all, if you're going to have a Fay Wray character being scooped up by King Kong, you certainly want a model to be able to look terrified, or at least a bit worried.

That has always been a problem with some models when they start out. They don't seem to want to smile too big or frown too much for fear of looking too wrinkled, silly, or unattractive. C'mon. What's sexier than a funny, pretty lady?

Eventually they come to a comfort zone and turn out to be great and a lot of fun. Of course, I have been backstage at some points when I realize that their egos have to be strongly intact to survive this job. One sketch required a model to crouch down inside a wishing well, and eventually stand up and walk around with the thing strapped to her. Not a graceful position, to say the least, and certainly not something she bargained for when signing up with a modeling agency. As she sat down in that well, waiting for her cue, trying to preserve what little dignity she had left, another model approached the wishing well, looked down into it, and said, "Hey, Jan, who's your agent? I'd consider a new one if I were you."

Auditions for our models are a test in self-esteem too. Every couple of months we do screen tests to search for a fabulous Barker Beauty. Nothing new to the business really, as just about every major star has been screen-tested early in their careers as well. It goes way back to old Hollywood, when the likes of Clark Gable and Katharine Hepburn were tested for their marketability and photogenic potential. But before all that, prospective models will send in their pictures to see if they can get an initial interview. If the pictures are decent, they come to *The Price Is Right* offices, put on a bathing suit, and do a little trial run right there in the corporate bungalow. It is a bit bizarre when you think about it, but if you're going to be in that biz, you need to surrender your embarrassment and humility at the door. Modeling is modeling, and not for the faint of ego.

If the producers like the initial interview, the interviewees will have the opportunity to have the aforementioned screen test in the following weeks. They will strut up onstage to music with someone announcing in the background to get them into the show mood. Then Bob, along with the other producers, will assess whether they make the cut. It's a little like a mini *American Idol* without the public castigation and without the caustic remarks of Simon Cowell.

We usually look for a variety of qualities. That's why you've seen a wide array of women modeling the show. Every ethnicity and look has been on the show, which keeps it all very interesting and diverse.

If you've been chosen as a Barker Beauty, you'll have many meetings and instructions from the director, and you'll watch lots of tapes of the show so you can get the hang of what we're looking for. The gestures done by TV models are essentially not natural human movements. I mean, really . . . when was the last time you stood there with one knee slightly bent in toward the other, a huge grin on your face, and flipped your hand up in the air like a trapeze artist who just landed on a mat? Guys, this really does require some training. We want them to look as at ease and comfortable as possible.

When it's all done, and they've appeared on the show for a while, they are put in a rotation with the other models, and will have regular appearances, do publicity shots with Bob, and if they're really fortunate, they'll actually get some recognition to the point of getting another gig here and there. Many a Barker Beauty has been seen in various magazine layouts, in an occasional movie appearance, and on a TV series now and then.

You may wonder how I know so much about the trials and tribulations of appearing on TV as a model. Well, with great reluctance, I'll tell you. It's because I've appeared on the show myself as, and I use the term very, very loosely, a model. Yes, folks, I actually modeled a few times with Barker's Beauties. And if you could harness the energy caused by my humiliation and embarrassment, you could have lit up Las Vegas for a month.

The producers thought it might be fun if the his-and-her raincoats offered as a prize were actually shown by a man and a woman. They had no male models, so they asked me to do it, and as camera-shy as I was, I still agreed, thinking it would probably be the easiest gig I'd ever done. After all, it was only going to be about twenty seconds on camera, a smile, a gesture, and off I'd go. How wrong I was.

During rehearsal I had a great time. No problem. It was very casual, and gave me such a false sense of security that I believed I'd be able to duplicate that calmness on air. There I stood in rehearsal with the raincoat, just cracking up, joking with the cameramen and crew, easy breezy. No problem. I could do this. I was going to be on the turntable with the model. No problem. She gave me some tips about acting natural.

"Just smile, look at the camera, then look at me as if you're admiring the raincoat, and look back at the camera," she suggested. No problem.

It was a problem.

Showtime came around and the makeup lady told me I should probably have some work done. Thanks, doll. Is my skin that bad? Wait, wait, of course. Television lighting is cruel. You need to look your best. Okay, go for it. Make my day. Make me up. After she applied the makeup, I almost burst into tears. I looked so beautiful . . . uh, good. "Dear God, why can't my skin look this good all the time? I look like a Cabbage Patch doll," I tearfully said to her.

As the stage manager led me to the dark and deceptively peaceful backside of that fateful turntable, I saw the model in the dim light waiting for me. She had a delightful maternal smile on her face that said *My little baby is going to be on TV. I'm so proud.*

I could hear the goings-on of the show on the other side of the turntable. I could hear Bob talking to the audience. I could hear the announcer bellowing out a new contestant's name. I could hear the loud cheers of the audience as the next contestant came on down. What I couldn't hear

*Gwendolyn Osborne*

was the pounding of my heart or the impending death knell of my career. Before I knew it, that turntable whipped around with the model and me on it, and what set in was a classic and totally unfamiliar sensation to me. It was the uncontrollable syndrome of stage fright. There it was, a big, ominous, robotic-looking Cyclops of a camera lens, right there in my face. The lights were blindingly bright, the audience applause and cheering seemed deafening, and I could see nothing but my own soul leaving my body. The announcer's words were received by my ears as "Blah blah blah blah blah." He could have been reading my last rites for all I knew. I froze. I started to shake and shudder. I tried to muster up a smile, but my bottom lip was trembling so much that I couldn't gain control of any muscle function that remotely resembled a grin or smirk or anything else for that matter. My face had become possessed by Satan. I looked like I was going to cry

*Rachel Reynolds*

*Gabrielle Tuite*

instead of smile, so I tried to ignore it as I followed the model's previous instructions. I looked at her raincoat, up and down, but as it turned out, I unintentionally never really made it past her chest, so it looked like I was gawking at her boobs. I finally looked up at the camera and in an attempt to stop my mouth from quivering, I unconsciously stuck my tongue *way* out of my mouth in sort of a *Blaaaaaah-I'm-scared-and-embarrassed* gesture. Yes, I stuck my tongue out on national television and didn't even realize it.

Before I knew it, I was back to the dark side of that turntable (and my future) with no model on my arm, and just a dazed look on my face. I was greeted by an equally dazed stage manager who asked, "Why did you do that?"

I said, "Do what?"

"Stick your tongue out on national television."

"Dear God, did I really do that?" I asked fraily.

I made my way back to the dressing room in what felt like slow motion—you know, the nightmarish kind where you say, *"Heeeeeeeeyyyyyyyy guuuuuuuuuyyyyyyyyys, thaaaaaaaaaaat wwwwwwaaaaaaassssssss aaaaaaaww-wwwwffffffuuuuuuuullllll."*

I came upon a gauntlet of staff and crew who stared at me in silence, their heads just slowly turning and following me as if I were a death-row inmate on his way to the gas chamber. Pity, disgust, and amusement were the sentiments at the moment, but all were in agreement that giving the camera a public raspberry was a no-no. As I reached the end of the gauntlet, there stood the producer, arms folded and looking down at me as he would a child who just broke his dad's favorite beer mug.

"Nice tongue," he said curtly, then turned and walked away.

*Shane Stirling*

*Lanisha Cole*                                                    *Brandi Sherwood*

"Great tonsils," said a crew guy. He walked away with a repressed chuckle, head shaking from side to side. How was I going to face the world after this? Holy humiliation! I blew it! All I had to do was stand there and smile, and I couldn't even do that. I wanted to turn in my CBS badge and die.

As it turned out, time healed all, and everything was forgiven. They even gave me another chance to appear about a year later, but this time the staff and crew did something to dig up the past while easing my pain.

I was so concerned I'd blow it again that when I appeared in a snowball fight scene in a showcase, right before the big door was going to open, several crew guys held up big cue cards, and written on all of them was "Keep your tongue in your mouth, Stan!" It got a good laugh from me and the rest of the crew, and never again have I stuck out my tongue on TV.

The point of this little tale was that I had a newfound respect for performers of any kind. Good models know their stuff, and just about everything in life is harder than it appears, even game-show modeling.

# 5

# HEARING VOICES
## The Announcers

**Imagine this:** One day, you're asked to read a lovely story in a quaint auditorium to a nice group of people. You have all their attention, and they are eager to hear what you've got to say, so you don't want to screw it up. Your focus is clear, concentration impervious. Then, all of a sudden, as you begin to perform your narrative, a man walks up to you and starts to recite the Gettysburg Address in your left ear. Next, a crazy lady walks up from the other side of the stage and starts screaming in your right ear, followed by 340 of her friends and relatives shouting behind her. To make things worse, there's this guy over in the corner who decides to blast his boom box with ten speakers and five subwoofers, completely drowning you out. This, ladies and gentlemen, is the hellacious life of a TV game show announcer.

*The first announcer on the show, Johnny Olson, was a class act and great legendary voice.*

One of the most underrated jobs on *The Price Is Right* is the task of announcing. This is yet another unique aspect of the show in that it is probably the most announcer-intense show on the air. So much material rests on the announcer, such as all the come-on-downs, all prize copy, and the occasional banter between Bob and him.

Announcers have a split brain. They wear a headset during the show and in one ear they're hearing themselves in addition to the actual recording of the program, and in the other ear, they're listening to a cacophony of voices and sounds coming from the director's booth. That, coupled with the crowd of yelling spectators, makes this a truly tough job.

In addition to all that, the announcer is also responsible for warming up the audience before we even start taping the show. It is hard to believe that this audience needs to be warmed up, but a TV studio is not a familiar place, and no one really knows how to behave.

Some instruction needs to be given during all this chaos, such as telling them not to chew gum on the air, when to applaud, and how to come on down. (No, that is not a natural instinct. You've seen enough people run right up on the stage, bypassing contestant's row.)

There have been many announcers on *The Price Is Right.* But only three have manned the post as a full-time job. In the early days, there was Johnny Olson. Johnny was a great guy. Everyone loved Johnny. His good nature was welcome everywhere. He was from the old school of Hollywood. Tough stock, yet a real gentleman to boot.

A more professional talent could not have existed. I had the honor of working with him for many years, and I kid you not when I say that I honestly cannot remember one single time when he made a mistake on the air. He was as smooth as silk, but then again, he had oodles of experience before he did *Price.*

For those of you who are facing the yearly renewal of your AARP card, you may remember that Johnny used to announce some classic shows like *Jackie Gleason's Honeymooners.* His voice was so distinctive that it became a voice that some would imitate, or at least attempt to. He did many of Goodson-Todman's game shows, like *Match Game, Tattletales, Password Plus, What's My Line,* and *To Tell the Truth,* to name a few. Johnny was also known for his perfect attendance record. Not bad for a guy who didn't even live in Los Angeles. He commuted from his home in West Virginia. (It was rumored that he had so much real estate, he owned it . . . West Virginia, that is.) No matter how sick he was, he would hang in there until the end. One time, he was so sick to his stomach that he had to throw up, so he just kept a trash can next to his lectern and barfed into it between "Come on downs." Now that's a trouper.

His audience warm-up was crazy. He'd come out into the audience with lights flashing and the popular disco song "Disco Inferno" blaring from the studio speakers. He'd run around, sitting in women's laps, rubbing his butt up against them, and making off-color jokes. The audience loved it, and it certainly set the party tone for the show that was about to ensue.

Not only was he a great announcer, but eventually he was used in showcase sketches as various characters. We would dress him up in drag, as Elvis, a baby in a carriage, and just about any other crazy character we could think of.

When Johnny suddenly passed away in October 1985, it was a great loss to the show both personally and professionally. He had done the show for thirteen years, and his face and voice were as much a part of the *Price* landscape as the big wheel and Barker's Beauties. We had many stand-in announcers, but the search was on for someone with the kind of personality that would be unique to the show and fit in with the festive and intense atmosphere for which *Price* was known. It was also important for the new announcer to have "listenability," that is, a voice that would not grate on you for an hour, because, as I mentioned before, the announcer has to talk constantly for the entire show.

After auditioning many really great announcers on the air for weeks on end, the final fit was obvious. Rod Roddy was chosen for a couple of reasons. He not only had a lot of experience, but he also had a bit of Johnny's tone in his voice, although he was by no means an imitation. It was surprising to me when I heard he was going to do the show because he was formerly the announcer on a prime-time hit show called *Soap.* It was as if he were an entirely different announcer on that show, because on *Soap* he was almost mellow in his style, whereas *Price* needed intensity and volume, and certainly stamina. This was just a testament to his talent and versatility.

The other reason that made him a good choice for us was that he seemed to work well as a character player in the showcases. With his funny animated grin, we had much pleasure humiliating him by dressing him up as ridiculously as we did Johnny. I'll never forget when he dressed up like Carmen Miranda, with a big, brightly colored Brazilian dress and humongous fruit hat. The audience cracked up as much as we did, and Rod LOVED it.

Rod became best known for one thing though. His brightly colored jackets were his trademark, and he even wore them when making public appearances. I used to call him the Doc Severinsen of *The Price Is Right.* Rod traveled to Thailand every year to scour the exotic fabrics of Asia, and had hundreds of jackets custom-made. He'd come back with the weirdest stuff sometimes, and I'd joke with him by saying, "Where the hell did you get *that* fabric, Rod? It looks like a clown exploded on you!" Many a Thai seamstress probably went blind sewing on the thousands of sequins that he'd have on some of those jackets.

Rod's audience warm-up routine was very different from Johnny's in that it had more of a Las Vegas opening feel about it, which was followed by a humorous instruction session that required the audience to stand up and take all these goofy vows. The "Oath of Audience," he called it. One was "I will not chew gum on television!'" and the audience would repeat, *"I will not chew gum on television!"* followed by a list of other on-air no-no's.

Rod loved the feeling of what he called "The Big Room." That's a reference to the important showrooms in Vegas where great talent would appear. He was crazy about big band jazz, so he had me scout for jazz albums, and I created a custom-edited grandiose brassy introduction track especially for him that would sound like Frank Sinatra was entering the room. He flipped when he heard it and used it for every show warm-up that he did.

"Come on Down!

Bob Barker

Some of the audience members would come to the show dressed like Rod, and eventually he was parodied on some comedy shows. I thought he would be hurt by one derogatory broad, goofy portrayal that they had of him, but the day after we both saw the satirical sketch, he told me he was completely flattered and loved being in the limelight.

When Rod was diagnosed with colon cancer, it didn't slow him down. He was just as much a trouper as Johnny Olson, in that no matter how sick he got, or how weak he was, he rarely missed a taping. He actually scheduled his chemotherapy around the taping schedule so that he'd have enough energy to do the show, with strategic timing of his chemo sessions so he'd have maximum recovery from the ravages of those kinds of treatments. You would have never known he was sick when he was at work. The only giveaway was his rapid weight loss, but he seemed to ignore anything that would remotely get in his way. He loved his job so much that he did it until he could barely stand the discomfort anymore. That's what is known as bravery.

After his seemingly endless battle with cancer, Rod passed away in October 2003. A memorial was given for him right there in studio 33 at CBS, with studio executives, celebrities, and friends attending the services in the same studio in which *The Price Is Right* is taped. It was very touching, and probably exactly where Rod would have wanted it . . . in the place where he loved performing so much.

Once again, after seventeen years of Rod's familiar voice, it was time to hunt for a new announcer. By this time the show was so iconic and huge that a deluge of announcers were beating down the doors. Everyone and his grandfather wanted the gig of the century. Our producer, Roger, let me listen in on numerous audition CDs ranging from famous announcers to complete unknowns. Being the star and executive producer, Bob Barker was, of course, going to make the final decision, but it was interesting to hear the immense diversity in style of these various voice-over artists. Many announcers were auditioned right on the air, just as we had done with Rod. They'd do a week or two of shows so they could get comfortable and receive lots of direction to show them off in the best possible light.

Before I get into the process of finding Rod's replacement, we need to travel back in time for a moment. (Once again, do you have your Intergalactic Spiratron Stratocruiser helmets on? Good. Here we go.)

*Rod Roddy was the second permanent announcer, and became famous for his outrageous wardrobe.*

The year is 1978. Johnny Olson is doing a warm-up and is goofing around with the audience. He asks if anyone out in the audience has any questions. A young, good-looking guy, about eighteen years old, stands up and says, "Yeah, Johnny, I've got a question for you."

Johnny answers, "Yeah, kid, what?"

The eighteen-year-old replies, "How can I get your job?"

Johnny laughs along with the rest of the audience and says, "You think you can do my job? Okay, come on down here!" Johnny then handed this kid the mike and said, "Let's see what ya got. Use my name, kid. Call my name down to contestant's row and see how you do."

The kid takes the microphone, scared out of his wits, and says, "Johnny Olson, come on down! You're the next contestant on *The Price Is Right*!" The crowd screams. They love it! Johnny, the consummate performer, pretends like he's all miffed, looks off into the wings, grabs the microphone away from the kid, and says, "Gimme back that microphone, kid, before Mr. Barker hears you backstage!"

That kid turned out to be our current announcer, Rich Fields. Yes, Rich had been an audience member decades earlier, and little did he know then that someday he'd be the full-time announcer on *The Price Is Right*.

Please reset your time travel dials to 2004. Thank you. (We know you have a choice of time-traveler pods, and thank you for choosing ours.)

*Announcer Rich Fields had some hard acts to follow, but has made the transition smoothly.*

After a plethora of auditions, it was eventually decided that Palm Springs weatherman Rich Fields would be a great fit. Rich had a smooth voice, and really didn't sound at all like either Johnny or Rod, but he was easy to listen to as well. (Remember . . . listenability.) Rich was a real pro with a lot of enthusiastic energy.

He's also a bit of a *Price* fanatic. He can be found hauling disposable *Price* paraphernalia like art cards and foam core cutouts from the set to his home at any given time. We tease him about it, but I have a feeling that his living room now looks like door 2 during a showcase.

Rich is having the time of his life. When he warms up the audience, it's a bit less formal than the previous announcers, but he does tell the story of his early visit to the show and the Johnny Olson incident. He does do something others have not, and that is bring audience members up onstage for a dance "contest" (with no real winners except for accolades from an applauding audience). It really gets the audience going and loosens them up a bit.

Of course, we have the great advantage of having the kind of audience that no one really has in the business, and that is a one-hundred-percent-participatory mentality. Everyone in that audience wants to be a part of the show. All are vying for attention in the hammiest way possible. I'm sure many of you have attended some sort of show at some time where the performers came out into the audience to goof off with some unsuspecting soul in their seat, either holding a microphone to their face or actually dragging their mortified bodies up onstage. The usual sentiment inside of people's heads is *Dear God . . . I hope that clown doesn't come over here and make a fool out of me!* You know exactly what I mean. You're the guy or gal who looks away, looks down into your purse, bends over to pick up a fictitious handkerchief that you didn't drop. Anything to get that clown to pass you up and avoid eye contact at any cost. Not the case with a *Price Is Right* audience member. Most of them are *offended* if they're passed up. They want to be seen in a big way, and they are more brazen than any spectators I've ever seen. What great chemistry that makes for a show! It's a performer's dream, and Rich takes advantage of every bit of it by getting an already hyped-up group and rousing them into a possessed frenzy. By the time videotape rolls and the show starts, the audience is so loud it is literally impossible to hear yourself scream.

I often joke with people who come back to the show multiple times to try out as contestants that it's a bad sign if they still have their voices. That means they didn't scream enough at the last taping. And then there are those who actually do lose their voices on their second or third visit and come back a day later to the interview with a completely raspy voice. Clearly they've had a good time, as they should. That, after all, is what this show is all about.

*Announcer Rich Fields works the audience into a frenzy before the taping.*

# 6
# MUSIC TO YOUR EARS
## Themes and Tunes

**PULL OUT YOUR EARBUDS** and pocket your iPods for a minute, kids, 'cause I want to talk about music. Not rap, not crossover country, not hip-hop, but *Price Is Right* jazz. You heard me. Jazz.

One of the other gratifying things I really enjoy doing on the show is supervising the music. I love it because it creates mood. I know, mood may be a slightly overstated portrayal of what's happening here, but a mood it is nevertheless. The mood ranges from excitement to laughter to glamour and even mystery.

Themes are themes. Most of them in television are accepted on their own terms, no matter how weird or unhummable they may be. You just get used to having them drummed into your head week after week, and *The Price Is Right* is no exception. Every-one seems to know the *Price* theme from our having played it a billion times over thirty-five years. We can't change it because it would be like rewriting the *Brady Bunch* theme or the "Tale of Gilligan's Island" . . . a pop-culture media blasphemy, to say the least. I was not involved with the original inception of the theme, but I did help develop most of the hundreds of pieces of background music played during the show today by meeting with various teams of composers and humming, describing, critiquing, and tapping on speakerphones with my finger for rhythm and pace.

There are over a thousand pieces of music in our library today. That includes all the specialty archive music that we use for showcases, foreign trips, or jukeboxes. The pure jazz-pop design of some of our stock pieces is so great that I still play music on air that was composed especially for us and recorded in the seventies. We've added tons of new stuff over the years, but there's no denying that the show has a distinctively loud and identifiable sound that is unique to *The Price Is Right* no matter what era the music originated in.

There are forty to fifty music cues (meaning occasions to play music) during an epi-sode of *The Price Is Right*. Everything is scored. Atmosphere must be added to all the prizes, sketches, and occurrences. As I mentioned in the introduction, most people are not aware that there's any music at all besides the theme. That's okay. You're not really supposed to notice the music. You're just supposed to unconsciously react to it.

In 1972, when the show was created, Mark Goodson commissioned a company called Score Productions in New York to do the soundtrack. The owner of Score, Bob Israel, who was known for some amazingly famous TV themes, hired a young composer named Edd Kalehoff to create a theme for *The Price Is Right.* He was an edgy young kid in his mid-twenties and had spent his teens and early adulthood in the sixties hanging around with well-known rockers in the biz, honing his musical skills playing various clubs and concerts with guys like Eric Clapton and Phil Collins. He came up with two themes for Goodson at the same time, *I've Got a Secret* and *The Price Is Right,* and both were recorded with a full band in London in the same sessions. He also recorded all the other background music for our show in those sessions (along with the theme for the 1972 Wimbledon tennis tournament).

If you actually listen to the *Price* theme, it has an unusual and complex melody. The one most impressive thing about the rest of the score is that it was totally unique for its day. Many other game shows had either a small live band on the stage, or the prerecorded stuff was often thin and rinky-dink. *The Price Is Right* was groundbreaking in its sound because Edd designed some hard-core jazz/pop/rock styles using a pretty hefty orchestral sound. Not only that, but it was coupled with a relatively modern instrument, the Moog synthesizer, the precursor to modern electronic music. Edd had worked with the composer John Barry on the latest James Bond film, so he knew how to create a sound that was full and intense, including impressive-sounding strings, woodwinds, and lots of brass. Rock-and-roll wah-wah electric guitars were used (à la *Shaft*) and every kind of percussion instrument to be found, from a triangle to chimes to snare drums. It was an expensive venture, but this was going to set the bar. Every ten years or so there was a new library of music added by various other composers in addition to Edd. Many of the oldies are not used anymore (much to the disappointment of the hard-core music fans of the show) because in a few cases it was just *so* incredibly dated that it felt odd to me, so I retired some of them. Much of it is still used, though.

Of course, the second most famous recognized and mocked piece of music on the show is what is known as the "lose cue." You know it. It's the one that is used whenever a contestant loses a prize. It uses the first four notes of the main theme, but has a goofy, tubby tuba as the lead instrument, followed by a trailing dissonant trumpet to give it a really distinctive *LOOOOOOSER!* sound. (Wah wah wah wah . . . brrrrrrrrrr.)

I have actually written showcases based on a piece of music I've heard. We subscribe to a couple of companies that have library source music for television and film scoring. You name the scene, you can find it in that library. From cartoon capers to classical to classic TV and film knockoff melodies, it's all there.

When I heard a piece of music that sounded just like the old *Dating Game* theme, I wrote a showcase that parodied that show. We created a duplicate set that looked just like the original *Dating Game* and the model was in go-go boots with big hair and asking questions, but instead of eligible humans, the *prizes* were the bachelors on the other side of the wall.

A *Green Acres* knockoff piece of music inspired a showcase, as well as a *Gilligan's Island* piece that we called "Finnigan's Island."

One of the funniest and most mocked pieces of music that we use was not specially composed for us at all. It is the yodel for the "Cliff Hangers" game.

*Our* Gilligan's Island *parody was entirely inspired by a knockoff piece of music of the original show's theme.*

It came from a very old Swiss yodeling album, and now it's so famous, we actually had a contestant volunteer to yodel for us on the air while she was playing the game. Bob asked me not to play the yodel when this woman said she could do it, so I didn't. Instead the eager lady playing the game actually yodeled while the little mechanical mountain climber moved up the mountain. It got a lot of laughs, and never before had I enjoyed *not* playing a piece of music on the show.

There is a whole faction of people who adore our music. I get e-mails all the time from people who want to know where to get our theme or background pieces. The theme is actually available on CD and online, but the other stuff isn't as easy to get. Our company uses the background music overseas in foreign shows, so they want to control the exposure it has to the general public and decided not to release it.

You'd be surprised how music is used by our fans. I recently had an e-mail from a fan saying he was getting married and wanted to play our theme as he and his bride were coming down the aisle. I told him that I hoped he would never need the "lose" music at any point in his marriage.

Many corporations request to use our music in their training. They'll do a *Price Is Right* mock-up and perform sales presentations while playing our theme. Schools, from elementary to college, love to play our music for either math training games for kids, or just a camp spoof of us for a dorm party or class presentation. There was even a disco version put out (not officially by us) that used our theme set to a disco beat that was played in clubs all over the country.

All in all, it's far more than meets the eye . . . uh, ear. Okay, I'm taking off the music hat now. Put in your earbuds and spin the ol' Podster to your heart's desire.

# 7

# THE GAMES PEOPLE PLAY

## Creating Our Pricing Games

## "I want to play 'Plinko'!"

How many times have I heard someone say that? Even when I'm not interviewing contestants, as soon as people find out I work on *The Price Is Right*, whether it's in a grocery store, optometrist's office, or the car wash, I hear people say, "If I got on *The Price Is Right*, I'd want to play 'Plinko'!"

The games people play on the show are part of the many vital elements that pump so much life into the program. We're like an amusement park that keeps adding, replacing, redesigning, and expanding its rides. It keeps people coming back for more, and makes it different on every visit. No two shows are alike.

The creation of games for *The Price Is Right* is a community effort, of sorts. The community actually started back in the seventies with the entire company of Goodson-Todman getting involved with creating new games. Mark Goodson used to have "New Games" meetings in the early days. All employees of the company were encouraged to create game ideas. They would do simple mock-ups and get fake contestants, usually other employees, to do a dry run of their game. Some mock-ups were as simple as cardboard, felt-tipped, paste-and-glue, macaroni, kindergarten-safety-scissors presentations. Others were complex, large, three-dimensional, life-size games with sound effects and lights. I was there for the pitch of "Plinko," which was created by then–executive producer Frank Wayne. It was based on an old arcade type of game called "Pachinko," which used a similar principle of dropping balls down a board filled with pins or rods. Frank brought in an old Pachinko board for everyone to look at, played the game for Mr. Goodson, and history was made.

Those pitch meetings were fascinating. Everyone would load into a small makeshift theater at our offices and Mark Goodson would enter grandly a few minutes late, like a king entering an arena, or a judge entering a court. A silence would fall over the group as everyone reverently anticipated Mr. Goodson's reaction to their presentation. All the employees, about forty or so, would be audience members as the games were pitched. There would often be a discussion among the group, and then the executives would leave the room to convene in the king's office. Within the next several days, all the "winning" games would be announced, and within a few months you'd see your game on TV.

Since Mark Goodson passed away, we're now left with only a small group of people on the staff who create games, although it's still open to anyone in the company who wants to pitch. Bob Barker has created some, as well as our producers, director, and several other staff members as of late.

There is also a graveyard of old retired games that just didn't work well, both conceptually and mechanically. No matter how many times we tried to correct the problems, it just wasn't worth the grief of having to stop the tape to reshoot a botched game play.

A good example was a game called "Professor Price." It was a mechanical type of robot, but looked like a middle-aged bald man, sort of scholarly. It stood there with its hand in an upright position. This was the only game ever created for the show that involved question-and-answer type playing, and not pricing, as all the games on the show require. This robot, or puppet, or whatever the heck he was, would hold up his hand, palm facing toward his face, and attached to this plastic hand were mechanical fingers in a closed-fist position. One at a time, as the contestant got answers right, he would raise a finger. There was a running joke around the studio that it was only a matter of time before there would be a mechanical failure and the good ol' professor would accidentally flip off the audience. That game was played only a few times until it was decided that it wasn't an appropriate format for *The Price Is Right.* So as it turned out, we virtually flipped off the professor instead, and that was the end of "Professor Price." Rest in peace.

Another defunct game was "Shower Game." It involved a huge set that had shower stalls in it, and contestants would stand in them, having either dollars fall on them, or the key to a car. Some people felt it looked a little, shall we say, distasteful, so the shower game got flushed.

Some games were so darned complicated that no one could figure out how to play them without some snag in the explanation.

There are tons of games that died, some quickly and painlessly, and some slowly and excruciatingly. I'm grateful that there were no funerals for all the games that were laid to rest, or I would have gained fifty pounds from all the deli platters at the wakes.

Here's a brief obituary of some of the dearly departed: "Add 'Em Up," "Bump," "Checkout," "Double Bullseye," "Double Digits," "Finish Line," "Fortune Hunter," "Gallery Game," "Give or Keep," "Hit Me," "Hurdles," "It's Optional," "Masterpiece," "Mystery Price," "The Old Balance Game," "On the Nose," "On the Spot," "Penny Ante," "Phone Home," "Split Decision," "Super Saver," "Superball," "Telephone Game," "Trader Bob," "Walk of Fame," and the graveyard just keeps growing.

*"Plinko" has gotten many a contestant out of debt with the mere drop of a chip.*

One of the games had a tragic back story. When the game "Cliff Hangers" was introduced (you know, the game with the mountain climber who yodels, which is also a favorite among many fans), one of our models, Janice Pennington, had recently lost her husband, Fritz, in a mountain-climbing accident. He was a professional climber, but never returned home, and hasn't been seen since. She wrote a novel about it years later. But, to add insult to injury, the nighttime syndicated host at that time, Dennis James, accidentally and unknowingly made a joke when the little mechanical mountain climber in the game started to climb and eventually fell off the cliff. "There goes Fritz!" he said, not realizing Janice's situation at the time. I'm not sure if it was left in for the airing, but there were lots of gasps in the studio from sympathetic crew members.

Although there have been a couple of games created that involve a physical skill, only one has survived. "Hole in One" (or the "Golf Game" as many people call it) is the

only game left that actually requires a person to do something skillful to win a prize, namely putt a golf ball into a hole. Bob has made this an opportunity to test his putting skills and get a couple of laughs as well. Before the contestant putts, Bob will try his very best to get it in the first shot. It became a

*Saving the life of our little mountain climber and winning a prize for it is essentially the theme of "Cliff Hangers."*

running joke on the set that, as soon as "Hole in One" appeared on the list of games for the day, the crew would get together to bet on Bob's putt. Even Bob would comment on the air about the pressure it put him under knowing that there were all these dollars floating around backstage hinging on this pivotal moment. Depending on whether he made the putt or missed it, you'd hear a resounding "AWWWWWWW" or "YESSSS!" behind the big doors, followed by wallets being pulled out of pockets and the ruffle of paper bills.

Bob frequently plays golf in his downtime. Well-known actor Adam Sandler, who is a fan of *The Price Is Right*, apparently knew this, and when he wrote the film *Happy Gilmore*, he created a part especially for Bob involving a now-famous scene in which Bob gets into a fistfight with Adam on a golf course. For those of you who haven't seen it, that scene alone was well worth the price of admission.

There is actually one game that requires a mental skill that is unique in the show. It also happens to be the only game that you can have a one-hundred-percent guarantee of winning every time if you play well, regardless of your knowledge of prices. It is the "Clock Game." This is the game that has two prizes, and you must bid on each prize, one at a time, after which Bob will say, "Higher" or "Lower," meaning your next bid should be higher or lower than the price you just bid. You keep bidding as fast as you can after each of Bob's responses until you get the price. Win both prizes, and you get a thousand-dollar bonus. Essentially this isn't really a pricing game at all, but a test of your skill to narrow down to a certain number between one and a thousand. Of course, knowing the general range of what the prize costs buys you more time and helps you to win faster, but getting there with a good strategy works every single time, even if you've never gone shopping a day in your life.

Trying to come up with new games is getting to be a bigger challenge as the years go on. Some games are revised versions of others, with a new name or look and some window dressing. Since it is getting harder and harder to impress a sophisticated audience these days, it was decided in 2000 that we needed something with an awesome punch. That game would be "Triple Play." This game has the potential for someone to walk out of the studio having won *three* cars. Each car needs to be priced correctly by bidding as close as possible every time without going over in order to win all three cars. Although it's not unusual to have someone win multiple cars on the show over the span of the hour, it certainly is unusual to win them in one fell swoop. The drama and excitement created by this game is unmatched by just about any single game we have on the show, with possibly one exception. That exception is "Golden Road."

"Golden Road" gets just about the biggest bang for the buck of any of the games. The reason is that we usually have a more expensive single prize at the end of the road than for any other game in the show. The contestant is required to bid on three prizes, which get better as you get farther down the Golden Road. Using numbers from the previous prize, you are required to fill in one missing number from the price each time, allowing you to move on to the next prize and eventually to the end of the road. This prize is usually an amazing car, like a Viper or Corvette, a colossal boat, or even a gargantuan motor home. It's loads of fun watching someone win the final prize because it really is a crowning moment.

*"Hole in One" is the most stressful game of miniature golf you'll ever play.*

"Golden Road" is always the first game we play on the show when it's scheduled. One reason is that there is so much setup for that game that it would be harder to do in the middle of the show while the audience is waiting. Golden disks are tossed on the floor, and three prizes need to be set, including the giant final prize, which is flanked by the large glittering rainbow set piece you always see. Which brings me to the perfect time to answer a question I've been asked once in a while by curious fans: At the top of the show, why does Bob sometimes come in through the audience and other times through the big door?

I'm sure many of you watchers may have noticed that Bob enters the studio from the back of the house on occasion. This didn't start as some random quirk or creative change they decided one day. It started because "Golden Road" took up much of the stage and couldn't be hidden easily. They decided to have Bob come in through the back, right down the aisle, and through the audience so the home viewer wouldn't immediately see that we were playing "Golden Road." The cameras were somehow able to shoot around all those huge set pieces until the contestant actually got up onstage to play the game.

Unfortunately, as the audience enters the studio before the taping starts, they are able to see the "Golden Road" set immediately, so it's no surprise for them. I distinctly remember when I started as a page at CBS (one of those red-coated usher types), I was seating the audience one day, and "Golden Road" was set up onstage. A woman walked into the studio, headed for her seat, looked up, and let out this bloodcurdling scream. I was ready to call 911 because she had sweat on her forehead, quivering knees, and the blood seemed to have drained from her face.

"Oh my God! They're playing 'Golden Road'!" she shrieked. It scared everyone around her, including me, but it was nice to know that a fan knew the show well enough to be aware of what was soon to come. It was also nice to know that someone wasn't having a heart attack.

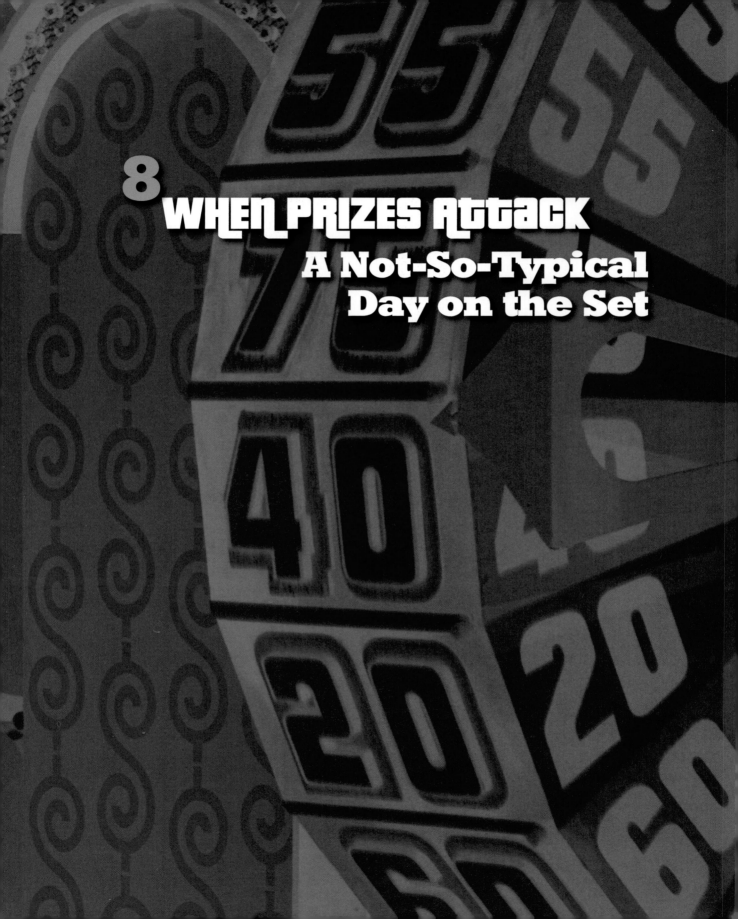

# 8

# WHEN PRIZES ATTACK

## A Not-So-Typical
## Day on the Set

**A WHILE BACK** one of our models showed up in tears because she'd just had a hair disaster at her private stylist's salon. Her hair was normally a warm blond, but it ended up getting so badly bleached she looked like Billy Idol. Then to compensate, she was dyed too dark, so she looked like Elvira, and finally it got burned so badly that it looked like red embers rising out of a rat's nest. Our hair stylist had to create a wig to imitate her real hair. Oh, the trauma of life in the lens!

When you watch the show, it seems everything goes smoothly, and that's the way we like it. After all, we don't want to come across looking like a junior high school talent contest. But no matter how hard we try, we just don't seem to be able to pull off perfection every single day of the year. I hope you'll still respect us in the morning.

That being said, I'd like to share some of the stories of our blunders and mishaps. There are plenty. Actually, some of the unusual stories that happen are not necessarily screw-ups at all, but just extraordinary things that happen on our set that are worth sharing.

I'll start with some of the scary stuff, like the attack of the killer models. No, not the latest B movie at your local theater, but living, breathing *Price Is Right* beauties who inadvertently turn into assassins. Some models have been unintentional weapons of mass destruction. For instance, when a car is shown, we occasionally roll it onto the stage by pushing it on instead of revealing it behind a door. This is a dramatic technique that is very effective, but if you don't carefully rehearse it, lives will be lost. We can't run the engines of any cars in the studio for a couple of reasons. One is fire safety. The other is that it would give away the surprise to the audience if they could hear an engine rumbling backstage. So what do we do? We get a whole slew of stagehands to push the car on in neutral. When I stand backstage and watch this, it's like a scene out of the movie *The Ten Commandments*. A bunch of people are lined up behind a car, and all at once, as if pushing a peasant cart out of Egypt, there's a symphony of grunts and growls as the SUV gets shoved out onto the stage from the side wings. The audience sees a smooth entrance, but the resulting hernias and ripping sound of back-support Velcro lives on forever in my mind.

Not only that, but the model who sits in the car and steers it onto its perfect spot doesn't always prove proficient as a driver. On more than one occasion, a model has confused the brake and the accelerator pedal. The resulting terror that ensues resembles an old Japanese horror film. Everyone goes running in all directions to avoid getting attacked by Carzilla and the announcer abandons his podium by leaping off the stage and into the audience before he gets plowed down.

I mentioned earlier about an exploding light bulb burning an audience member. No one can really help that. What you *can* do is hope that a special effect goes well. We had rigged a bucket of water above a door once, which was supposed to dunk a model with a splash as she walked through it at the end of the showcase. We did the showcase, she walked through the door, and *nothing.* Everyone onstage, including the special effects people, scratched their heads. Apparently there was too much water in the bucket, making it too heavy to tip, so we had to go back and reshoot it later, but the spontaneity was lost. Out of context it made no sense to the live viewer, and the audience scratched *its* collective head.

Since we have new models all the time, there is a great deal of new material for them to learn. It's not just about gesturing and fondling refrigerators, as I mentioned earlier. They have to know how and when to reveal prices during various games, as well as turn lazy-Susan-type devices for small items. Playing a game recently, we had two models at a rotating table on a game called "Joker." As Bob asked them to reveal the next small pricing item, each model decided to turn the table in the opposite direction, resulting in a reverse tug-of-war, more like a push-of-war. This gave Bob some comic material, as he just walked over and said, "Ladies, you seem to be wanting to turn that thing in opposite directions. Why don't I just count down, and you can turn it *that*away. Ready? Three, two, one, GO!" This got a good laugh out of the audience, and caused a nice shade of blush on the models.

The calling of contestants can be a real challenge from an accuracy point of view. We have a master list of all the names of every single person in the audience, because when the time comes, John Smith and John Smyth sound exactly alike. Or even John Smith and Joan Smith. Or John Smith and John Criss. I've seen people try to pull a fast one and run down when their name is John Barton, and when we ask them why they came on down, they say, "Because my name is John Chris Barton, and John Smith sounded a lot like John Chris." Nice try, buddy. Now get back to your seat and turn up your hearing aid.

I can't count how many times we've had people come on down with similar names, or a Junior and Senior who got mixed up. Nothing is more humiliating than running down on a nationally broadcast television show and being told that you're not the one they wanted. (We should probably have a psychiatrist in the audience standing by for those 331 people who aren't picked to come on down.)

I once had a traumatic experience myself with this in the days before I picked contestants. I was asked to get special tickets for a friend of a friend of a friend's manicurist's gardener's maid's aunt. In other words, I didn't know who the heck this person was, but it was a favor. These special tickets make them ineligible as contestants, and so they didn't have to wait in line, and they had special guest seats taped off for them. I met the guest, Billy Trumball, and his wife before the show, greeted them briefly, and explained that they would *not* be called down due to their special guest status. They nodded and acknowledged the comment, and proceeded to their reserved seats.

The show started with the usual uproarious shouts and applause, and all of a sudden, the announcer said, "Billy Trumball, come on down!"

*Holy crap!* I thought. *What are the odds of that? There's another friggin' Billy Trumball in the audience!* Sure enough, my guest leapt to his feet, and came on down, along with the other Billy Trumball, the one who was really supposed to be there. We had to stop tape and fix the confusion. Apparently, *my* Billy thought we were surprising him by telling him that he wasn't eligible, but called him down anyway as a favor. Folks, that's a resounding NO, NO, NO! That will never happen. It's illegal, verboten, shunned, and for those who speak Spanglish, el-wrongo.

Mark my words, whenever I have special ineligible guests now, I tell them the Billy Trumball story and say, "I don't care if they call your name, I don't care if they point at you, I don't care if there's a five-thousand-watt electrical charge under your seat. If you hear your name, keep your damn jumping-bean ass in your seat or I'll come down there myself and smack you over the head with a nine iron!" It's never happened again.

Prizes occasionally have their temperamental mood swings as well. During one of our prime-time shows, we played "Lucky Seven," a game that requires a car to be pushed onstage on the air in the same way I mentioned earlier. We had a really expensive Cadillac convertible to roll on, but when the show started and it was time to push the car on, it wouldn't budge. The car was so electronically sophisticated that it went into a shutdown mode because the key fob wasn't nearby and the car wouldn't release its antitheft device. Everything froze, including the producer's heart. The audience sat and waited patiently as we had to read the instruction manual, shake the car, kick it, yell at it, and pray. Without this car, the show could not go on. It was placed in a position that prevented a huge portion of the show from being staged. It felt like a stubborn burro refusing to budge out of principle. "I'm just not ready!" was what this defiant little candy-apple-red curmudgeon was appearing to say. Eventually someone thought to call the local Cadillac dealer and beg someone to come and fix the problem, but the longer you wait, the more restless the audience becomes, so that seemed more like a plan B. Eventually they got an expert on a cell phone and talked the crew through various steps to get it out of park and into neutral. This caused a burst of applause from a wary audience, and a great desire by all of us to bring back into production the 1976 Ford Pinto so that we'd never have to deal with modern electronics again.

One of the worst things that ever happened on our set was the severe injury of one of our models, Janice Pennington. At the opening of every show, Janice used to hand off the microphone to Bob standing at the edge of the stage, which rises about three or four feet above the audience level. One day we had a new cameraman, and he wasn't aware of Janice's vulnerable position on the stage. Right after Bob is introduced on each show, that one camera swings around and catches a shot of the audience. It's a fast move, and the camera swung around as it was supposed to, but the enormous lens at the front of the camera knocked Janice right off the stage headfirst and down onto the concrete floor below. It caused a concussion that knocked her unconscious for a while and tore ligaments in her shoulder that never recovered entirely.

One of the things no one can predict is politics and world tragedies. You may think that these events don't affect us, but the year that Hurricane Katrina hit New Orleans, it made news around the world and caused programming problems for us. Even though we're usually on top of that sort of thing, we accidentally aired a show with a trip to New Orleans as one of the prizes. Since the shows are taped weeks in advance, these kinds of things can slip through the cracks. We had many letters of complaint from angry viewers who thought it was insensitive and inappropriate to give away a trip to New Orleans right after it was practically wiped off the map. It was an unfortunate mistake, but, I assure you, not intentional, and surely forgivable. We apologized to as many callers as we could.

Another big political song and dance was when the Iraq war started and France was not siding with the United States. You remember all the anti-France stink that happened, I'm sure. French fries were banned across the country, and freedom fries were put in their place. (Amazing how much alike they tasted.) Not only that, but the sentiment in France toward Americans was not in the least bit warm and cuddly. We were about as welcome there as a skinhead in a synagogue. As a result, it was decided that we better not send anyone to France or it would look like we were handing over our contestants to a firing squad. I don't think anyone noticed really, but we didn't give away trips to France for years.

When some German tourists were killed in Egypt, we ended our Egypt trips. When the terrorist train station bombings happened in Spain, we pulled our Spain trips. The World Trade Center attack put a major damper on all travel for a while, but eventually we started sending people to New York again, because we felt they needed the good publicity as a city. Shunning a major American city like New York for an extended period of time would have been unpatriotic in some sense. Supporting their economy and image was as much an effort of rebuilding as any of the local efforts that were happening, so we tried to reincorporate East Coast trips as soon as we could. The same went for New Orleans. We eventually aired the New Orleans shows that were held back earlier.

We don't have many wardrobe malfunctions, but we do have contestant malfunctions. While I'm interviewing potential contestants, I always take into consideration the physical ability of the person. We're pretty flexible with all that. If you can speak, you can pretty much play most of the games. One particular day, I picked a great feisty older woman who was incredibly animated both vocally and in her arm movements. I was totally taken with her, and immediately knew I wanted her on the show. I moved right on to the next interviewee and didn't give it another thought.

When the show started, we called her. "Gracie Yavanovitch, come on down!" The camera panned and panned, looking for good ol' Gracie, and after a few moments, she slowly emerged from the crowd of screaming faces. Unfortunately I neglected to take note of this sweet lady's inability to walk easily. No sweat really. We've had people in wheelchairs, people with broken legs, fractured arms, all of it. All okay, except at that moment, I looked down at my notes and saw that we were playing a game called "Bonkers," which required a bounding sprint back and forth across the stage with a time limit. The moment that I realized that, I think I lost several years from my life, as well as a tuft of hair that just leapt from my scalp. Let's face it. Even though this isn't a stunt show with obstacle courses that need to be conquered, in reality you can't have a ninety-year-old woman with a cane running back and forth during "Bonkers" (or our other running game, "Race Game," either).

I came flying out of the audio booth and down to Roger, the producer. As soon as it sank in what the situation was, he had as much of a panicked look on his face as I did. We were either going to have to stop taping and set up another game for her to play, which meant a long, arduous, boring stop-down of the show, or pray that she didn't bid well enough so she wouldn't get onstage.

The game-show gods were on our side, and she didn't get onstage, but I did call the local mortuary to start digging my grave. I reassured everyone that this would never happen again . . . I hope.

And speaking of contestant malfunctions, one of the things we discovered is that it's really hard to "come on down" when the contestant isn't there. You heard me right.

On more than one occasion, a contestant got called down, but no one responded. Everyone just waited and waited. One time the contestant finally showed up at the back of the studio, frantically coming through the door after her friend raced out to inform her that she'd been called. When she finally realized what was going on, she was quite embarrassed. She reeeeeealy had to go to the restroom. When ya gotta go, ya gotta go. Sorry to say this, but one of the worst things you can do at a *Price Is Right* taping is go to the bathroom. Hold the Big Gulps, guys!

We love unusual prizes. That's why we once decided to put this great group of furniture made out of clear Lucite on the show. Wow, what a novelty. What a creative choice. What a bungle. We made the unexpected discovery that putting clear Lucite furniture on TV as a prize was a bad idea. Why? BECAUSE IT'S INVISIBLE, EINSTEIN! YOU CAN'T SEE IT! DUH! How embarrassing for us was that? We ended up having to put tape around the edges of every piece of that furniture, otherwise we'd open up that door, and we might as well have said, "Yes, it's a new . . . nothing."

Don't laugh at us. We meant well.

A most amazing occurrence that happened was during a commercial. A woman in the audience with extremely long hair said that she wanted to donate her hair to a charity that makes wigs for cancer patients. She asked Bob if he'd cut her hair off. He agreed, and when we came out of the commercial, Bob took a scissors, sliced off all this woman's hair, and handed it to her right there onstage. It was a very cool moment, both for us as a show and for the woman who would donate the hair.

Inanimate objects also have an evil life of their own. Many a refrigerator has tipped over on a model. Many a price has revealed itself at the wrong time. Many a trip wall has come crashing down to the hard concrete floor. Many a basket with jewelry has flown in too fast and swung back and forth like Tarzan's vine. Bob once struggled with the revealing of a price on a game called "Squeeze Play." Apparently he'd had enough of trying to get the panel to drop, so he did a major karate kick to get the damn thing to open.

*Bob cuts off a woman's hair to give to a cancer charity.*

Sometimes it's not a mechanical problem, but a pronunciation problem. Associate Producer Kathy Greco and the prize department check to see if everything sounds good with the product descriptions while they're being read in rehearsal. Occasionally, we need to take special note of how a product's name is pronounced. A product spelled "Homedics," which is pronounced "Home Medics," can easily be announced on air as "Home Dicks" if someone doesn't catch that in rehearsal, and would surely have the audience wondering what kind of product it is.

Of course there are pronunciations that just can't be controlled, and no matter how much we rehearse it, if a contestant slaughters the product's name, so be it. Like the time when a contestant with a heavy accent looked at a bag of Tidy Cat litter, and called it "Titty Cat." I'm sure the sponsors weren't thrilled, but it made total sense to soften the "i" in that word, since in many foreign languages, it would be pronounced that way. There was a debate whether to keep it in the show, and it was decided that we should, because it was natural and real. Hey, stop chuckling! I know you are. Okay, so did we. For days.

One of the cool things about rehearsal is that it's very casual, but still serious business. Sometimes we'll have a moment of insanity, and for laughs, the models and stage managers will collaborate to play a joke on the rest of us. The most morbid and dramatic joke was when we rehearsed the showing of a car. The doors opened up, and sure enough, there was the car as usual. The only thing that wasn't usual was that the models had lodged themselves in all sorts of contorted positions all over the car, as if a horrible accident had just taken place. One model was facedown, crammed under a wheel. The other was sprawled out facedown on top of the hood. The stage manager had opened the door slightly and just hung his limp hand out at the bottom of the door. The announcer just went ahead and read his copy for the car, and when he was done, door 2 slowly closed as if nothing was wrong, and the "bodies" didn't move once the whole time.

Occasionally when there's a new model, the crew likes to scare the hell out of her. When we've given away freezer chests, a couple of stagehands have been known to hide inside and when the model would open up the chest during rehearsal, the guys would jump out and the screams could be heard as far as Nova Scotia.

Of course, a chapter on an atypical day can't end without the most talked-about moment from the show. This had to be one of television's first real wardrobe malfunctions. It was none other than the famous Yolanda tube top incident. For those few of you who haven't heard of it, you'll want to know that Janet Jackson had nothing on this lady.

As Johnny Olson called down a contestant named Yolanda, she came out of the audience faster than just about anyone I'd ever seen. Her energy was so frenetic that she almost looked as if she were being electrocuted. She was shaking and bouncing so much when she came on down that her tube top came on down too, and she stood in contestant's row completely bare-breasted. She didn't even know it had happened until our production assistant Sarah, who sat in the front row during tapings, leaned forward and told her. The audience went wild, and when Bob Barker came out, he was under the impression that the uproarious cheers were for him. When he addressed Johnny Olson about it, Johnny said, "Bob, they have given their all for you."

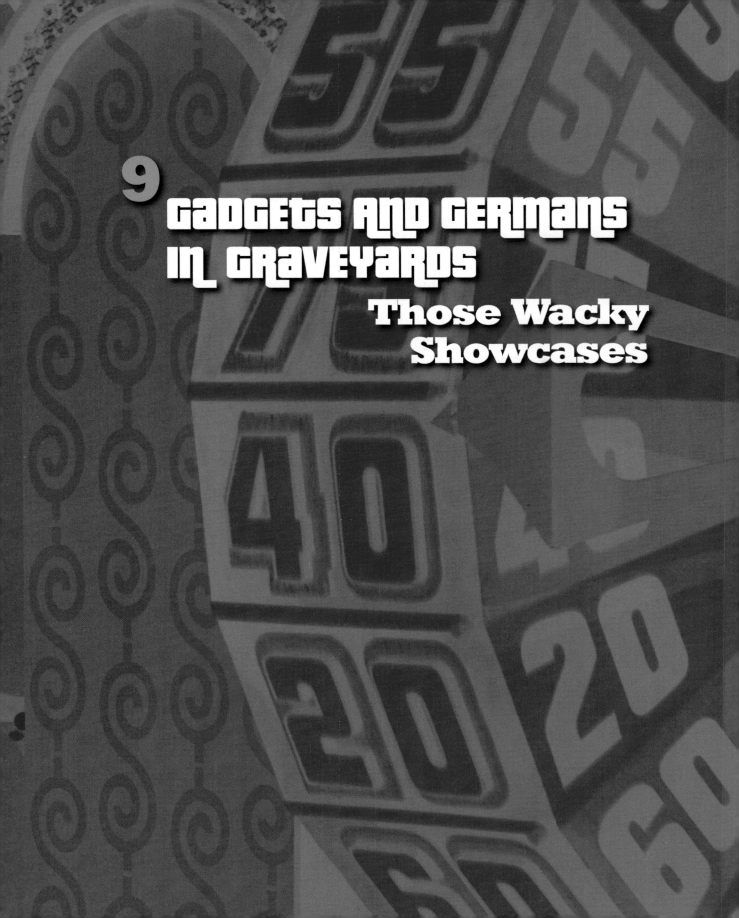

# 9
# GADGETS AND GERMANS IN GRAVEYARDS
## Those Wacky Showcases

**the PRICE IS RIGHT** is like a big, juicy, delicious buffet. There's a little bit of everything for everyone. You want a little competition? Just watch the bidding among the four contestants in contestant's row, and you'll see raw bidding fights with one-dollar one-upmanship bids that will piss off even the kindest of little old ladies. You want a little sex appeal? Just watch Barker's Beauties modeling for a spa or a water vehicle. I've known people to watch the show just for that (not to mention Barker's sex appeal to a vast audience). You want violence? Well, you've all probably seen Bob getting clobbered by a contestant or two. You want reality TV? There isn't anything more real than an un-coached contestant going bananas after winning a sports car.

Yes, your hunger for entertainment will be satiated with merely one viewing of the show. And if the main part of the show is the meal, then the showcases are the dessert . . . the thing you wait for at the end of the meal that you've been looking forward to for the entire dining experience. Showcases have the sweet taste of success written all over them. That's because, when someone wins it, it means they've arrived. They've done something few people in the world have a chance to do, and that is win, and win big. Winning a car or an African safari is still a big deal, no matter how jaded you are by million-dollar prime-time windfalls. And on *The Price Is Right* they have to work for it. It's pretty clear that good bidding throughout the show will pay off for a savvy contestant. Even though the spin of the big wheel is a lucky element, contestants who play well during the main part of the show are given the advantage by spinning the wheel last, which increases their odds of getting into the showcase.

There are two kinds of showcases: stock and special nonstock. The stock showcases are your usual living room/dining room/playroom offerings without a story or sketch attached. They pass a parade of prizes your way with any combination of items. Sky's the limit on these. (Or should I say, "Budget's the limit"?) They can end on just about anything, including motorcycles, cars, boats, trailers, or just a trip or piano.

The nonstock showcases are an odd bit of television-making. They usually end with the big-ticket items. Imagine having to do funny little sketches, tell a story, incorporate

*The sky's the limit as far as showcase themes go, and we've done 'em all.*

prizes into that story, and do it all in less than two minutes. Since we do several of these sketches a week, they take an unbeliev-able amount of planning and time to create. It's like putting on a superfast hypercaffeinated miniplay every day. Some of the special showcases are simple, sparse language concepts with no sets and no costumes, but rather a series of art cards or verbiage like "Fun in the Sun," "Garage Sale," or "Ways to Get Wet." But a few times a week, we go hog-wild and do a major burlesque routine.

When I create showcase concepts along with my writing partner and the show's edi-torial consultant, Adam Sandler (no relation to the actor who got pummeled by Bob Barker in the film *Happy Gilmore* but who cracks me up no less), we try to come up with ideas that are fresh, quick, funny, entertaining, and goofy, with one eye on story and the other on prizes. It looks easy, but after thirty-five years, every concept in the world has been done to death, and there are times when I stare at my computer and think, "Oh God, there isn't a new idea left" But then, like an anvil falling off a cliff onto Wile E. Coyote's head, something new conks me in the right brain, and off I go. Remember, our little stories have a beginning, a middle, and an end, usually with a little "tag" at the very end of the showcase that nicely ties up the story with a joke, a consequence for the character, or a silly prop gag. These stories have a set formula that the viewer is, albeit unconsciously, familiar with in rhythm and style.

Oh, by the way, future contestants, when deciding about the first or second showcase, there is no rhyme or reason as to which is the bigger, better showcase. For some reason, a contestant will pass on the first showcase, even if we've offered them a Trump-size yacht and limo, a genie in a bottle, and a shopping spree at Fort Knox. That kind of strategy is usually followed by a resounding groan from the audience. Hey, our devious job is to challenge you! We don't want you to know what's coming, so sometimes the big bang happens for the first showcase, and sometimes it's the second. Sorry, all you know-it-all game-show junkies!

The showcases have had a very dramatic change over the life of the show. In the earlier years, under the supervision of the original producers, the showcases were sometimes five minutes long, and were huge, complex productions with fire and brimstone, swashbuckling sword fights, and collapsing buildings. The models had speaking parts, the announcer played characters, and it took ages to rehearse. As the show got further along, everyone realized that, because Bob was so entertaining with the contestants, why not shorten the showcases and allow more time for banter during the body of the show? This turned out to be a great streamlining of the show and gave Bob more time and less pressure to rush things along during the hour.

Adam and I meet once a week to pitch ideas to each other and work out details of concepts that we've prepared during the week.

"Do you think we can do a showcase about a billionaire bunny named Floppy, dress a model up in a bunny suit with an ascot, top hat, and cane, and have it travel the world?" I enthusiastically ask Adam. "And he can line his cage in thousand-dollar bills, and . . . okay, get this . . . *island hop! Get it? Island hop!*" (Stupid hardy-har-har laugh follows.)

He liked it. I liked it. Why not?

We usually agree on most stuff, but we occasionally need to pull the reins on each other, so we act as good sounding boards during these meetings.

We eventually have to go and pitch all these ideas, no matter how crazy, to the producer, Roger. He'll either yea, nay, or revise the language or concept. Roger usually gives us tremendous creative leeway and lets us get away with a lot of goofy stuff with little quarrel.

But occasionally . . .

"What do you mean, you don't like a billionaire bunny?" I bark at Roger. "We think it's cute! We think it's funny! We think it's genius!"

Roger didn't. Floppy was dead.

One of my favorite showcases was a Halloween showcase we called "Graveyard of Prizes."

It came to me one day as I saw an old horror film on TV. All these corpses rose out of their graves fully dressed but all dirty. I thought, *Why not do this with showcase prizes and famous characters?* So I thought of three famous historical people whose names I could mess around with. One was Scarilyn Monroe, another was Ludwig von Schmutzhoven (for those who don't know Yiddish, *schmutz* means "dirt"), and finally

*The "Graveyard of Prizes" showcase was a small Halloween epic to produce and scared our executives in charge of the budget as much as our viewers.*

Aristotle Oasis. I thought it might be really fun to actually have them rising out of their graves, but how could I do that without killing the models? After all, I had to bury them for several minutes until the big showcase doors opened up and their cue to rise out of the grave came from the stage manager. This is where the *Price Is Right* shortcut creativity comes in.

Obviously, we couldn't cover them in dirt, so I asked our special effects department to build three shallow boxes that the models could lie in. The whole graveyard would be covered in brown artificial turf that would be laid over the boxes and in front of each gravestone. The turf would be split in the middle of each "coffin" box, and be able to be thrown back like a bed sheet so that it would look like the characters were emerging from the grave.

Then I went to our costume designer, Robin, who was going to make the famous white Marilyn Monroe dress, but all messed up, which of course would be fitting for a dead person. The "Beethoven" and "Onassis" outfits were to be decrepit too. They were all covered in powder and dirt so that when they stood up, they'd have dust flying off of them like old, stale corpses. I spoke to the makeup person, Carol, about making them all pale and dead-looking. Our hairstylist, Mira, would make some great wigs and fill them with dust, so every detail would come together to create a really great haunting effect. Our special effects department filled the stage with fog, and I put some eerie music onto the soundtrack to add to a great Halloween mood.

The premise of the showcase was that these corpses were unhappy being in their graves, and wanted something more out of their lives . . . uh, deaths. Scarilyn Monroe was tired of having a dirty, skimpy dress, and craved a new washer and dryer, so she had one hidden behind her gravestone. Aristotle Oasis was tired of being cold all the time and felt that the cemetery folks should supply him with a portable fireplace near his grave. Ludwig von Schmutzhoven said he'd had enough of life underground and wanted to live above it, so he left the cemetery and would spend eternity in a new trailer. (I wanted to make a Beethoven "de-compose" joke in the script, but it was rightfully nixed.)

I occasionally enjoy watching evangelical TV shows on Sunday mornings, mostly because they are filled with drama, slick production, and are quite entertaining. I watched a preacher waxing philosophical on what it takes to get into heaven. As he spoke in tears and grand platitudes about what pleases God, I wondered if, during the Pearly Gates screening process, Saint Peter had a sense of humor when all these people showed up to try to get into heaven. Does he have rigid standards, or is he so sick of all the excuses that he merely lets people into heaven with a joke or two? Oftentimes when we create show-

*The "Angels in Heaven" showcase was a humorous look at what it takes to get through the Pearly Gates.*

case scripts, we use puns and jokes endlessly to lead to prizes. This showcase was no exception. We put an echo into our announcer's voice to play the part of Saint Peter. The Pearly Gates set was huge, and our angels had gold fabric wings that were custom-made for the showcase.

In the script one of the reasons the angel would give Saint Peter for her entry into Heaven was that she never illegally downloaded anything on her MP3 player.

Saint Peter says in a booming voice, "That isn't good enough. Try again, doll!"

She then pleads her case by saying she once helped a little old lady cross the street while she was visiting Rome.

Saint Peter replies angrily, "You call that a good deed? Humbug! What else ya got?"

Cowering, the angel says, "Okay, how about this. I watched *Price Is Right* every day."

And of course, *that* deed miraculously opens the Pearly Gates as we hear a resounding refrain of the "Hallelujah Chorus" from Handel's *Messiah* and it gets her onto the shuttle waiting behind the gates that would take her directly to heaven. And of course, the shuttle was a brand new minivan. The tag at the end of the showcase was the angel slapping a big sign on the side of the minivan that said, "Shuttle to *T.P.I.R.*," insinuating that the show itself was Heaven on Earth. I know. Shameless self-promotion. It's what we people in TV do best.

There was a hair of controversy on this one. We had a letter from a person who felt that playing the "Hallelujah Chorus" in this context was blasphemous. Didn't we know that it was a sacred piece? All I knew was that George Frideric Handel was not necessarily anything but a composer sitting at his piano hammering out a great tune. I don't remember him or the piece being ordained by anyone. Heck, I just thought it was funny in the showcase.

One other letter felt that our reasons for getting into Heaven were clearly inaccurate, and that it should have been obvious to everyone what the real prerequisite for entry was. Two complaint letters. Wow. Call the National Guard. We've got a riot on hand. Maybe it wasn't *that* controversial, but we are constantly aware that no matter what we do or say, *someone* will be offended by it. There are probably people who are offended by the mere notion of giving away prizes at all.

A truly inspired showcase that Adam created was called "Pluto's Protest." Some of you may remember that the planet Pluto made the news because scientists decided that it no longer qualified by definition to be a planet. Some of us on staff had a debate about how strange and funny it was, and of course,

*The "Pluto's Protest" showcase turned out to be quite the wardrobe challenge to both the designer and our model.*

all's fair in love and showcases, so it had to become a showcase theme. Adam came into the writers' meeting with this idea that we ought to dress up a model like the planet Pluto and have her protesting her change in status. In the background would be a field of other planets, and she'd be holding a sign that said, "I'm number nine!"—of course referring to Pluto being the ninth planet. The story would be that Pluto is so pissed that, if demoted, it would not allow the use of its name for that famous dog who resides at Disney World. And if demoted, it would do its best to block the view of Neptune so no one could see it through their telescope. And the final punishment for its demotion would be that it would consult with its good friend Mercury, and convince Mercury to never allow any car company to use that name for a new car. For the tag at the end of the showcase, poor Pluto ultimately didn't get its way and a scientist in a lab coat stormed in, angrily grabbed Pluto's protest sign, and broke it over her knee, marching off in disgust.

The costume for this character was amazing. It required the special effects department to create a huge foam planet that a model could wear and still move around in while holding a sign. The costume designer put her in a leotard to match the foam planet, and it would have to be suspended and dropped carefully over her head.

The showcase turned out great, and everyone on the set seemed to get a big kick out of it, as evidenced by the grins across the stage and in the audience.

The other challenge with all this is that we've designed these showcases in a way that allows us to do set and costume changes without stopping tape for long periods of time. Remember, we tape a one-hour show in just a bit over an hour. There are several good reasons. Once again, we never want the audience to sit and wait for hours since they are such an integral part of the mood and liveliness. The other is to save money. Every minute that ticks by in a TV production costs cash for the studio and the crew, and this being a business like any other, cash savings rules all. Incidentally and equally as important, we don't want to wear out Bob Barker's energy either, because during the commercials, he talks to the audience, and endless stop-tapes would wear any host down for over an hour.

So next time you watch the show, imagine that during the commercial, while you're getting pitched toothpaste and mildew cleaner, we're out there backstage breaking our butts like a live Broadway show, changing the entire look of the set. Dozens of people are rushing around as if in a fire drill. Commands are being barked out by stage managers, backdrops are being flown in, prizes placed, hair is being ratted, noses powdered, clothes are whipped on and off, and all because of our deep, devoted, undying, eternal, dedicated, superlative commitment to keeping 340 people from getting bored and fidgety . . . Oh yeah, and the money thing too. Now aren't we the magnanimous ones!

# 10

# LONG DAY'S JOURNEY INTO PRICE

## Stories of Traveling Contestants

**PEOPLE GO TO EXTRAORDINARY LENGTHS** to make their dreams come true. Coming to watch a taping of *The Price Is Right* is no exception. It shouldn't surprise me to what extent people will go to haul their families, friends, and coworkers out to California to see this show, but it often does.

Given that some of these people have ruined their lives to get here, I thought I'd ask them about their travels and goals concerning this show. Why do I say ruin their lives? Think about it. Some students are missing class and thus flunking exams and thus becoming really bad doctors or nuclear physicists, and thus affecting my next visit to a hospital or nuclear power plant. C'mon, would you want to go to a doctor who missed the class about heart transplants because he spent the day trying to win a refrigerator? Or the gal who ditched the plutonium purifying seminar to win a case of acne cream? Perhaps an exaggeration? I don't think so. Next time you go to have open-heart surgery, ask your doctor if he or she knows how to play "Check Game." If he or she says "yes," run like a bat out of hell!

I went out onto the line at CBS and asked people to tell me about their escapades before they got there. Some of them ran up to me and started immediately spewing out stories like an excited child sharing an amazing anecdote that couldn't wait to be told. Others wrote about it on a sheet of paper I supplied them with earlier and eagerly handed it over like a confident student turning in their aced exam. Here are some stories of people's experience before and

*Patsy decided to get attention by breaking her leg in nine places when she fell off her scooter while mailing a ticket request to us.*

during their visit to *The Price Is Right*. Try not to feel too sorry for them. They had a good time when they got there, and some went home having won a new car.

§ § §

**Stacy** told me that she was naked just a few hours ago. Not unusual, as we're all naked at some point in the day. But she was naked at CBS Television City. Why?

*This morning on the way here, a hot cup of coffee spilled on my new white clothes. I had to strip in the bathroom and wash my pants and shirt. To get the stain out, I was wet and cold, but that's okay, because I love Bob!!!*

Stacy got on the show and was an awesome contestant. No one knew how wet she was.

§ § §

One fellow named **Alan** decided to tell his adventure in the form of an article. He was there with a group from a restaurant called Chili's, and they all had this story to tell. Apparently Alan felt it was his big chance to exhibit his journalistic skills, in addition to his heroic prowess, so he wrote this:

*Another night of insomnia, mixed with anticipation, led me to believe dawn would never arrive. I lay unconscious finally at six thirty a.m. before I hear the alarm barking at six forty-five. I rush to meet the group at Chili's in Northridge to start our adventure. As we are about to set the course, we hear a loud bang. A car crash in front of the restaurant. This causes a loud blaring of a horn as a man lay unconscious in the wreckage. With instinct as my wings, I flew into the restaurant, grabbed the fire extinguisher, and ran to the car. We pulled the man out, turned off the car, and doused the wreckage. The ocean of fluids never went ablaze.*

As a follow-up to Alan's story, **Merritt**, also from the restaurant, decided to do a little plug to amend the story.

*We saved a man from a burning car and still made it to* The Price Is Right *to see*

*Bob. That man is able to watch us come on down now thanks to us! We really do serve up a good time.*

Who knew that being saved from an exploding car by an unknown hero would have such great rewards as attending the taping of a game show?

§ § §

Then there was **Laura**, who actually loves the show enough to sacrifice property, her relationship, *and* an animal.

*As I was getting ready to go out my door this morning to come here, I locked my keys in my boyfriend's car and my precious love bird Trudie, who runs free in my house, got out! Well, I could not be late to meet my group, so I broke the window of my boyfriend's car and grabbed my keys, took my own truck, and yelled out, "Good luck, Trudie! Don't get eaten! Gotta go!" Hopefully I can find my bird, and I know I will need a new boyfriend.*

Sorry, Laura, we're not giving away any new boyfriends on the show.

§ § §

Our audiences get to us in almost any imaginable way. I interviewed some students who rummaged around in trash bins to collect aluminum cans so they could raise money for gas to drive out here.

Another visitor was a maid at the Hyatt, and saved her money faithfully to come see the show. She said she'd clean rooms, but only clean the bathrooms during the commercials so she wouldn't miss the show.

But not until now did I realize how much the term *death benefit* applied here.

*My sister and I had to wait two years for an elderly lady to pass away. (We were her caregivers.) We then cleaned out another elderly lady's apartment to raise enough money to get here.*

Hmmmm . . . I believe we now may need to make our show mascot the vulture.

§ § §

Here's another one who couldn't wait for the Grim Reaper to knock on her friend's door. **Dorothy** had dreamed of coming to our show for years, but being the gracious caretaker that she was, never could escape long enough to come out to LA.

> *I took care of an elderly lady for twelve years before she died and I could be away from home for a few days. She finally died at the age of ninety-three. Then a friend of hers, at eighty-four, needed help . . . Stuck again.*
>
> *At least now I could get away. I don't know any more old ladies! At least older than me.*

Thank God for the limited human life expectancy. Otherwise no caregivers would ever be able to come to our show.

§ § §

Quite often I interview people who have prevailed in spite of horrific odds. Most of them are cancer survivors who are either currently on chemotherapy, facing it, or have gotten past it, living with fingers crossed from day to day. It becomes a real revelation to me that one must do everything one can to enjoy life, and not put off the things one has been aching to do. It really touched me when I heard about mother and daughter **Tracy** and **Jeri**.

> *My mom and I do everything together. In 2002 we both found out that we had cancer. We've always been* Price Is Right *fans, so we decided then one of our goals would be to get on the show. It took us four years to get here (from Minnesota) but they were four cancer-free years, and we made it!*

Congratulations, you two. Here's to many more visits to *The Price Is Right!*

§ § §

This story, told by **Sara**, proves that the prize of true love is a ticket to *The Price Is Right*.

> *I came to the show due to many coincidences. Two weeks ago, I met a man, and now we're dating. Then randomly met his friends who happened to have an extra ticket to the show. So I traveled in a car from San Francisco with almost complete strangers, which has actually been one of the craziest and fun times of my life.*

LONG DAY'S JOURNEY INTO *PRICE*

Clearly your new friends are people of tremendously good taste. I say you marry the guy.

$ $ $

Okay, some stories are just too cute. **Margaret** must have been a precocious little child.

> *When I was only four years old, I would hold a jump rope in my hand and pretend I was Bob. All the kids on the street would be my audience.*
>> *"Mawgwet Subweezie, come on down!"*
> *I even broke my mother's car antenna pretending it was Bob's microphone.*

Mrs. "Subweezie" . . . I beweeve we owe you one antenna, wight?

$ $ $

It was a particularly warm November day when **Benjamin** decided to sweat it out in a tux and come to our show.

He had the option to nurture magic and romance by dancing the night away at a school event, but instead decided to hightail it over to CBS.

> *I came out to LA and missed my senior black and white formal to see Bob. I even wore my tux and brought the boogie to Bob.*

$ $ $

Anyone know what a schlemazel is? It's Yiddish for "hopelessly unlucky bastard." Meet **David**.

> *I drove all the way here from Connecticut and even though one of our cars blew up in St. Louis, we ran out of gas in Utah, and had to work shameless hours with no pay for the tickets, I'm still here. I even had to suffer getting my ticket revoked the last time I tried to get in.*

Welcome to show business, baby!

$ $ $

Ditching school doesn't pay. And yet **Hilary** felt tragedy was the angle to take in order to get here.

*I e-mailed my anthropology teacher at the University of California Santa Barbara that I got in a severe biking accident yesterday so I could be excused from my midterm in order to receive a kiss from the one and only Bob Barker. Yay!*

Nothing worse than a lying australopithecine-like Homo sapiens who's no better than an anthropoid hominid and could revert us culturally all the way back to the Pliocene Epoch. Don't know what that means, Hilary? Yeah, we know. You missed that day.

§ § §

Not exactly sure what the motivation was for the naming of this person's houseplant, but **Georgia** seemed to think it was appropriate.

*My great-granddaughter gave me a Venus flytrap and she named it Bob. So every day, I have to water Bob to keep it alive.*

Hate to break it to you, Georgia, but you need to rename your plant. The real Bob is a hard-core vegan.

§ § §

**Tamesha** is a real trouper.

*Well, on my flight here to LA, something told me that my credit card was under the limit. I got to the hotel and the attendant said it was over the limit. So I had $30.00 to my name until some money was wired. I used it for a taxi ride here at 12:30 in the morning. He put me out half way here and I walked the rest of the way. I slept on the sidewalk just to become a contestant.*

Two pieces of advice for your next visit, Tamesha: 800 numbers work better than psychic intuition to determine your credit limit, and the next hotel you stay in should be half the distance from the studio as the last hotel you stayed in.

§ § §

**Mesia** got a taste of the LA streets that few people get to experience.

*While I was waiting for bus 14 to take me to Beverly Boulevard, two cars pulled up to the curb and asked "If I was working."*

*I said, "Working? What does that mean?" After a few seconds, I said, "No, I am waiting for the bus." The funny thing is that I had on blue jeans and a sweatshirt. What kind of "working girl" wears that? I told the people that I met in line and they said, "Wow, you love* The Price Is Right *so much, you're willing to be a working girl for a night."*

Shame on you, Mesia, for looking so damn good in sweats. Tone it down next time.

$ $ $

Here's another guy, **Zachary**, who hung in there for us.

*Long ago in a studio not so far away, my grandmother was a lucky contestant on* The Price Is Right. *Although she didn't win her game, she did win a wardrobe for a newborn child. That newborn child was me! I have come here today to carry out her legacy and win the game that she was not fortunate enough to win herself.*

I thought I noticed during our interview that your clothes were a bit snug. Time to dump the layette, Zach.

$ $ $

**Hayley** had some bigger goals than winning a car when she came to see the show.

*I traveled all the way from Austin, Texas, to propose marriage to my honey, Bob Barker. I have an engraved ring and everything. I must meet my love.*
*XOXOXO*
*Haley Drews (soon to be Barker)*

That is *so* sweet . . . SECURITY!

$ $ $

Not that I'd like to portray LA as this crime-ridden, prostitute-laden town, but I couldn't pass up **Valerie**'s story for sheer positive attitude.

*This morning at 3:30 A.M., we left two of our party in line while Heather and I started to look for a place open to buy coffee, etc. A few blocks away, we located a 7-Eleven. After our purchase for our group, we exited the store. Two men came up from behind and told us to give them our money and keys to our SUV. Nervous and scared, we were in the process of doing as told when the store manager ran out with his gun screaming at the muggers who then turned and ran away. The police were called and when we leave today's taping where we hope to be called to "Come on down" by you, we will "Go on down" to the police department to finish our report. But looking on the bright side, we could have been "Laid on down" by the muggers.*

Thanks for the clever tie-in, Valerie. Remind me to have you around for a good laugh during my next shoot-out.

§ § §

We have a very important, life-sustaining function besides sheer entertainment, as **Bella** has pointed out.

*When my daughter called to tell me that we had tickets to attend* The Price Is Right *show, I asked her how I was ever going to remember to take my 10:00 a.m. medication without Bob's smiling face and his invitation to come on down! She replied that I would just have to attend the show and ask Bob myself. So here I am and I am happy to say that I even remembered my 10:00 a.m. medication.*

Bob Barker alarm clocks will be available in the lobby.

§ § §

All I have to say about this following letter by **Staci** is "When all else fails, fall back on *The Price Is Right.*"

*I was fresh out of college and at my first job interview with an accounting firm. They asked me if I had any special skills. I told them I always thought I would make a good Barker's Beauty. I then got up and did my best "hand swoop" to the pie charts on the wall. Although the rest of the interview was serious, they remembered me afterward as "the* Price Is Right *girl," and I eventually got the job.*

We're there for ya, babe.

§ § §

For those of you concerned about the undying dedication of our health care system, **Stacy**'s story may make you think twice the next time you check into your local hospital.

*(We) nurses worked a 12-hour night shift. At the end of the shift, a young boy coded and we had to hurry up to save his life so we could get to the taping of* The Price Is Right. *We went through San Diego and Los Angeles rush-hour traffic and ran a mile from the parking garage to the studio in stilettos without stopping to pee once. You'll be glad to know the young boy is still alive and we made it to see Bob!*

Nothing worse than a spike-heeled, full-bladdered, life-saving frenzied nurse.

§ § §

At first it sounded like **Jolyn** loved her husband's gift for their wedding, but read into it a bit. You may sense something else.

*What's the best part of a wedding? The honeymoon, of course. And who/what better to celebrate with than Bob Barker and* The Price Is Right? *Most men woo their women with romantic sunsets and candlelight dinners. Not Mike. He surprises me with 5 a.m. wakeup calls and Barker's Beauties.*

Bitter, party of one! Bitter!

§ § §

Blame is an ugly thing, **David**.

*I missed my flight because I was watching* The Price Is Right *in one of the Dulles Airport pubs.*

Uh, David. I don't know how to say this. Wow, I'm really uncomfortable right now, but here goes . . . Uh, are you sure it was *The Price Is Right*'s fault and not the 10:00 a.m. martinis?

§ § §

We get a lot of military people visiting our show, which is great, but we didn't realize what a tough decision and sacrifice some soldiers make. That pivotal moment came for **Robert**'s friend . . . country, *Price*, country, *Price*.

*I am a lieutenant in the Air Force stationed at Los Angeles Air Force Base in El Segundo. I was extremely jealous of one of my comrades in arms when he told me the opportunity he had to go on* The Price Is Right. *At the very last minute (last night actually), a higher mission of extreme priority surfaced and he sacrificially volunteered for temporary duty in support of a greater calling. I vowed to take his place as a contestant on your show. I represent my brother in arms today and will contribute half of my earnings on his behalf.*

Thanks for serving us in every way, Robert! (And your comrade too.)

§ § §

Here's another soldier, **Karen**, from that same group who was grateful to attend a taping and made us a priority.

*I'm here with a group of your fans from Los Angeles Air Force Base. Seeing your show live has been a dream of mine since I was about eight years old. So when I heard of the opportunity to come here today, I was thrilled. My coworkers are launching a GPS satellite into space today, aboard an Air Force Delta II rocket. But as fun as launching rockets is, being here is an even bigger blast. I'm counting down until you say, "Karen Cole, come on down!"*

Next time you get into your car and you get bad directions from your car's navigation system, feel free to direct all complaints to our show.

§ § §

Oh, how times have changed.

*I've been watching* The Price Is Right *since 1972 and I always wanted to appear on the show and give Bob a hug and kiss. Now my husband says he would like to hug and kiss Bob also.*

**Maria**, you've been watching our show for a long time and we thank you, but darlin', if I were you, I'd start watching your husband.

§ § §

There's nothing quite as tragic as a starving artist. **Thomas** will attest to that.

*I am the advance catering chef for the Rolling Stones. If my boss knew I was here instead of shopping for the largest show of the tour, I'm sure I would be fired. The show's at Dodger Stadium and I believe I would be sent home. I did it all for you, Bob!*

I thought Mick Jagger looked a bit gaunt when I last saw him. Shame on you, Thomas.

§ § §

A bathroom, a bathroom, my kingdom for a bathroom.

*I got a $937 fine for Bob. After we got out of our car and it was not parked in the vicinity of a bathroom, in a random alley, I ran over to a bush and urinated. A policeman happened to be walking down at the end of the alley and ticketed me for urination in public. We then, as a group, ran to the CBS building so we wouldn't miss our group spot.*

Perhaps you'll win some bladder panties on the show today, **Jordan**.

§ § §

Congratulations to **Donna**, who has found a great antidote to overeating.

*I lost 239 pounds so that I could sit and fit in the seats on* The Price Is Right. *I love Bob more than food!*

The *Contestant Diet Book* will also be available in the lobby.

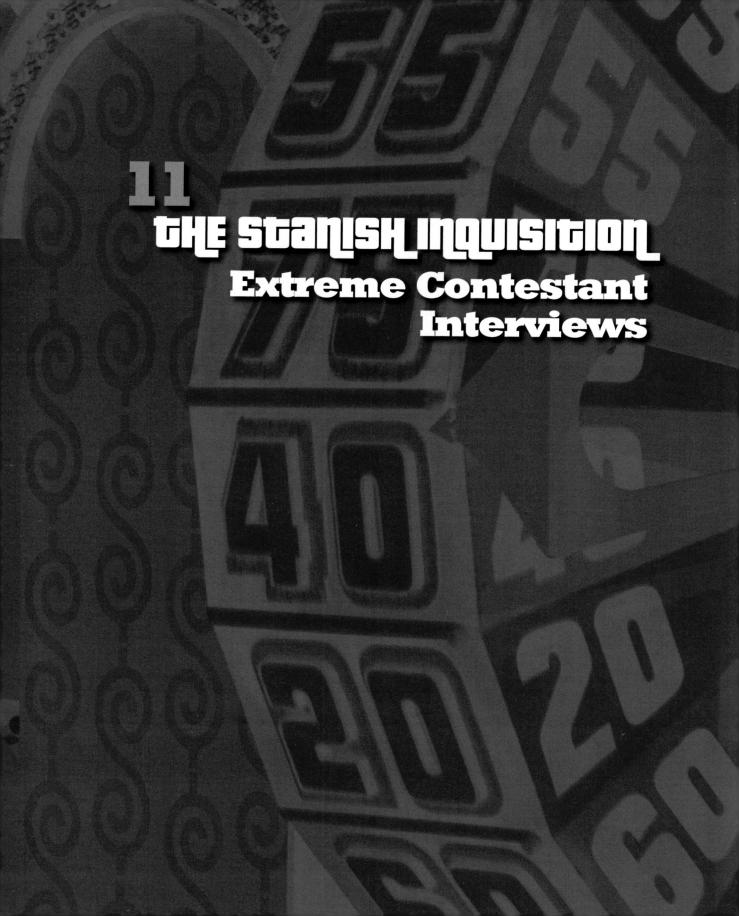

# 11
# THE STANISH INQUISITION
## Extreme Contestant Interviews

**I am the PERFECT PERSON** to be a contestant coordinator. Why, you ask? Because I am the Carlsbad Caverns of curiosity. The supernova of nosiness. The crown prince of prying. The more I know, the more I want to know. I must know everything about everyone at every minute, so don't even *try* to keep things from me. "None of your business" isn't in my vocabulary, because everything *is* my business! I love information, and that's that.

In my job I spend a good portion of my day feeding my insatiable appetite to know things about everyone and everything. I get to ask lots of people lots of questions and it only feeds the wild beast of data inside me. Best of all, it gives me perspective. And because of my inquisitive nature and interrogative obsession, a coworker once described a conversation with me as "The Stanish Inquisition."

It sounds like an amusing job, and it is, but interviewing 340 people in an hour and a half is harder than it looks, especially if you're dealing with a swelteringly hot day, which can produce a lackluster audience. Do the math. That leaves only about fifteen seconds for some people, although to me, it feels like a lot longer. Often I'll spend a minute with one and seconds with another. It's a pounding pace, and my energy level has to stay the same for the entire time so no one feels they've gotten the short end of the stick. It's also a mood elevator for them if they enter the studio feeling good and excited, like they have a fair chance to get on the show.

Even with a great audience, there are a few guidelines that I've been given by Bob Barker who, in addition to being the star, also happens to have the official title of executive producer of the show. After all, he's the one who ultimately has to deal with the contestants up onstage, and the more material I can feed him, the more fun he'll have, and the better the show will be.

It can take its toll to try and mask any angst I might have during the interview process, but I try to do it with humor and speed, and hopefully no one on that line will even know what hit 'em after it's over. It may be freezing cold outside, or hotter than Death Valley, which doesn't exactly help someone to be their "true self," especially when compounded by the fact that they've been out there for hours, sometimes as many as twelve or more! In any case, it's my job to see through all the shivering, fanning, disgust, exhaustion, and nervousness and dig down to their souls in a matter of seconds.

Oddly enough, no matter what the conditions, the audiences seem to love it. They request free tickets online at the CBS Web site, and are processed by CBS pages when they arrive. Their names and social security numbers are taken and quickly typed onto a master list. This allows us to do a quick background check on them. No, we don't know if they're felons or escaped convicts (and trust me, a few have looked it), but we can tell if they've been on a game show in the past several years and whether they're eligible to be on our show. There are legal limitations as to how many times you can appear on a game show. Who knew?

All audience members are given a nametag and a number to stick underneath their name. After processing, everyone lines up outside the studio on miles of aluminum benches. After several public-address admonishments such as, "If you've got a logoed T-shirt, turn it inside out, no mention of products or companies on air, no funny hats or costumes, no cameras, no fistfights," etc., they are ready to "audition," as it were.

A couple of hours before the show, they are lined up about twelve at a time in front of me behind a red railing. I'll pace back and forth in front of them like a drill sergeant

*This mob has been interviewed, and is ready to enter the studio with great anticipation . . . and relief that the wait is over.*

(without the in-your-face screaming and cussing) and quickly ask each of them a few questions like, "Where are you from, and what do you do?" I'll joke with them or make a silly comment about their job to see how they'll respond. Sometimes I'll be talking to one person, but watching another out of the corner of my eye because people are often more honest and let their guard down when they don't know they're being watched. Hopefully in those first moments, they'll show their best side. Production coordinator Scott Schalk

takes notes during this process. He sits behind me on a director's chair and writes feverishly the entire time we're interviewing. Usually, it's a quick note that may include a physical description as well as highlights of my conversation with these potential contestants. Sometimes it's just an outstanding word or phrase, like "shaved head . . . Mr. Clean look-alike," or "Giggly and pent, professional light bulb installer." He makes it look sporadic, and doesn't always write something immediately, so don't think you can tell what and who he's writing about. He's very sneaky that way.

*The audience loads in right after the interview, and each and every one of these people awaits his or her destiny. Retro-dance music keeps them clapping and energized before the show.*

Some of you may have heard of "speed dating." It's a contemporary phenomenon of finding a mate by attending a social somewhere loaded with eager singles. The procedure is to spend two minutes with someone sitting at a table, and then moving on to a nearby table to do the same for the next person, and the next and the next. Sounds like an insane way to meet a life mate, and perhaps it is, but it works beautifully for our intentions on *The Price Is Right.* We are, of course, not looking for life mates. But we are looking to fall in love with someone for a few minutes within the hour, and for my purposes, love at first sight is totally possible when looking for contestants. True, it's not a deep, long-lasting love. I don't want to buy them dinner or pick out china patterns at Bloomie's, but it is extraordinarily thrilling to meet someone whom you instantly get excited about the moment you meet him or her. That is the ideal scenario. Sometimes I just settle for extreme "like" or just measured tolerance instead of love if I can't find the latter that day. Dear God, it actually occurred to me once that I was looking for the same qualities in a contestant that I would in a first date: sincerity, energy, and humor. Who wouldn't want that? It's what works best for contestants in almost any game show.

So think of the interviews as speed dating. You know who you like. You know who you love. You know who turns you on, and you know who is going to be good on the show within moments of meeting them. And remember this, oh great fakers of the world: It has nothing to do with jumping or screaming. It also hasn't anything to do with looks, race, age, hairstyle, ability to cheerlead, shirt slogan, or that cute stuffed animal that you shove in my face. It just doesn't. I've fallen in love with lively senior citizens who exude charm and joy, as well as big burly construction workers, people with major disabilities, and cocky, floppy-haired, goofy, nerdy college students. And a great personality doesn't always rear its feisty head immediately. Sometimes it takes a bit of coaxing, but with a little effort, most personalities show through if I set the stage for them.

As I make my way through the entire line in this manner, I will probably have about twenty or thirty people in mind who are potentials. About thirty minutes before the show, I'll go into the studio with all the notes and we'll hash out the pros and cons of each prospective person, carefully narrowing it down to the final nine people who we think will be great contestants.

It's a nerve-wracking moment for me, because quite often, I'll have two or three good people who may have a risky element to their personality, perhaps quirky or sassy, and I've got to pick one based on my gut feeling. That can translate into either a great moment on the show, an absolute deadbeat who totally shuts down, or worse yet, someone who pisses everyone off by hemming and hawing during one of the games.

I've had the wool pulled over my eyes a few times (those who watch the show a lot will know exactly what I mean), but in all cases it's given me tons of material to think about, and certainly to write about.

There are days when I have so many people I like that I wish I could put them all on the show. The bad news is that I can pick only nine. The torment of not being able to pick someone that I'm nuts about is a killer for me. And I know that some of them will never come back to the show, so that is it. They're the ones who got away.

Because I couldn't put them on the show, I thought I'd start off by sharing some of the great interviews I've had with people who almost made it by the skin of their chinny-chin-chin, but were, nevertheless, as amusing and wonderful as they could be in the interview. I've also put in a few who were *not* in the final cut at all, but cracked me up, or just plain puzzled me. I have kept them all anonymous to thwart those who were potentials from slashing their wrists knowing that they almost made it onto the show. Mostly though, the names were changed . . . to protect me! (Nothing is worse than a pissed potential contestant.)

## The Ones Who Got Away

It's a Monday morning and I'm about to undertake the task of interviewing 340 people for *The Price Is Right* taping that day. As I approach the beginning of the line, I see the eager faces of those who have been standing out on the line since two in the morning, some in sleeping bags, some stretched out on metal benches like med school cadavers. Getting there early had never guaranteed their being chosen to appear on the show before, but at least it got them into the studio that day.

Frankly, I'm amazed that any of them have enough energy to speak, much less give an energetic performance during their interview. After all, the Pavement Posturepedic bed doesn't exactly make for a restful night.

But there is not even a semblance of exhaustion in any of them ever. Quite the contrary. They seem to be energized by the moment of truth, so to speak. They perk up at the prospect of actually having the interview that could get them a new car, or perhaps a case of anti-itch ointment.

Some people look really familiar, and that's because they have shown up to this interview dozens of times in the hope of getting picked. I can recognize most of the repeaters right away, and on occasion, we'll get a joker who has actually been picked to come on down before and thinks he or she can get on the show again, even though they're clearly told ahead of time that they can't. There's a rule that prevents you from doing that. I have gotten down to mere minutes before the show, and after the background search, I find out that they're ineligible. Since years can go by before these villains return, and since I will have seen some fifty-gazillion people since, I usually don't remember them, or they were picked by someone else years before I did this job. These people are sneaky. They'll switch a couple of letters in their name or go by a nickname when filling out their eligibility form, change their hair color or wear glasses, but ultimately their social security number exposes them as the frauds they are! Just a warning to those who think they can outsmart us. We know who you are, and our crack background research detectives will track you down like dogs in the night, take your firstborn, and tattoo an "R" on your forehead (for "repeater"). If you try to get on this show twice and deprive someone else of winning a car, you're just a big ol' prize hog, and you will be attacked in the parking lot by people throwing cases of Preparation H and other consolation prizes. Point made.

The anticipation is considerable on the part of both the folks in line and myself. Scott and I approach the front of the line, and often they'll burst into a cheer or applause, either because they've figured out who we are, or they're just glad the waiting is almost over and they can get on with it.

The first twelve march themselves in front of me, like facing a firing squad, as one contestant so aptly pointed out, and face me with big smiles on their faces.

I look the first person straight in the eye, and with the loudest, most invasive tone I can muster up, I shout, "Hey there! Welcome to *The Price Is Right*! How the heck are ya?"

## Diapers

Edith graduated from the June Cleaver University of Housewives. Very proper, in her fifties, a hairstyle that is a throwback to the seventies, and a conservative dress with a sweater draped over her shoulders.

"Hi, Edith! How are you today?"

"I'm fine, thank you," Edith says with polite restraint.

"Where are you from, Edith?"

"I'm from Minnesota. But I'm not here for myself. I'm here for my son," she says in that typical Minnesooooota accent.

"What's the matter, Edith, don't you want to win a car?" I ask curiously.

"Oh, well yes, uh no, uh," she stammers while looking over at her son. "I mean, that would be lovely, but he would be much better than me, oh yeah, he would. Ya see, he's been watching since he was just a little baby. 'Come on down' were his first words. I couldn't tear him away from the TV. Even if he had poopy diapers, I'd have to let him just sit there all stinky until the show was over. The only difference now is that I don't have to change his poopy diapers."

I turn to the son and notice that he's completely mortified. He's got that typical teenage I-don't-know-this-woman-please-kill-me-now look on his face.

"Brandon!" I shout to the embarrassed boy. "You changin' your own poopy diapers now?"

Without making eye contact, he smirks and quickly says, "Yeah, whatever."

"You're totally humiliated right now, aren't you, Brandon?"

"Nah, it's okay, whatever," he says with a little bit of a snicker.

"Well, Brandon, promise me that if you get up onstage, you won't make poopy undies in front of Bob Barker."

The group laughs, the kid loosens up a bit, and I'm standing there thinking how many thousands of teenagers across this land are embarrassed by their parents. Should *any* parent talk about a child's bowel movements in an interview, or anywhere else for that matter?

## Yee Haw!

"Howdy, Stewart!"

"Howdy, Stan!" he says with a drawl as he looks at my ID badge. Stewart is about six foot five, in his sixties, with a bulbous red W. C. Fields nose that I'm sure has dipped into a beer mug or two.

"Where ya from, cowboy?" I ask with a slightly mocking Texas accent.

"Ahm from Austin, Texas. But you probably already knew that 'cause of mah ten-gallon hat," he says as he tips his hat briefly.

"It's not the hat that gave it away, Stewart. It's the shirt that says 'Don't mess with Texas.'"

"Well, now I reckon that would o' helped too."

"I see you're here with a large group. What's the group you're with today?"

"Well, some of us are related, and some ain't, but we all dun come out here to see *Truth or Consequences.*"

"Well, that's going to be pretty hard, Stewart, 'cause that show's been off the air for over twenty-five years!"

"Oh, dear Lord," he grunts as he realizes his mistake. "Ah meant *Prahs Is Raht.*"

I laugh and say, "I figured that, Stewart."

I loved this guy's accent and wonderfully rich character. You just knew that Stewart had lived a good full life and enjoyed every minute of it.

## Dying to Come on Down

"Hey, Spencer, what's up?" I say to this pasty-looking kid.

"How you doin'?" he answers with a cocky nod of the head.

Spencer is about twenty-eight, and has a mischievous smirk on his face. His closely cropped black hair and roundish moon-shaped face has black horn-rimmed glasses perched down on the lower part of his nose. He is pale, and this gives him a goth edge that I find fascinating.

"Where ya from, Spence?"

"Buffalo, New York."

"What do you do, Spencer?"

He says with a familiar whisper, "I seeeee deeeaaaad people."

"Lousy way to make a living, wouldn't you say?"

"Not if it involves embalming and makeup."

"So you're an embalmer? Wow. You're my first dead person handler." I focus in with true interest.

"I'll give you my card." He adds with a morbid grin, "Give me a call, or better yet, have your relatives give me a call on your behalf if you need my services."

"I think I'll hold off for a while, Spence. So do you like your job?"

"I love it," he says with a lighthearted tone, which gives me a bit of a chill. After all, what is it that would make a person *love* working with dead bodies all day? It makes me realize that one can truly be desensitized to almost anything one is exposed to if around it long enough. I suppose being around death all day is no stranger than cutting open a live body and transplanting a heart, or a cosmetic surgeon sucking the fat out of someone's ass.

Amazingly though, every mortician I've interviewed since absolutely loves his or her job.

## Reach Out and Don't Touch Somebody

"Well, well, well, who have we here? Joanelle?"

"That's me, honey! The one and only!" she says with a sassy edge.

Joanelle is a big, buxom, beautiful African-American woman in her early thirties. She's dressed in a very colorful lilac print dress and has teased-up hair almost reminiscent of a style you might see in a sixties high school yearbook picture. It looks odd on a woman so young . . . makes her look way over forty.

"Where are you from, Joanelle?"

"Richmond, Virginia."

"And what do you do?"

"I'm involved with a church group that goes around the country promoting abstinence. Our motto is 'Have the romance, but keep your thingy in your pants!'" she says proudly.

"That's pretty funny, Joanelle. Tell me, are you really concerned with what people are doing with their thingies?" I ask with slight bafflement.

"You betcha, baby. We think you crazy men ought to control your big bad selves," she says with hands on hips followed by a deep whooping hyena laugh.

I look down at my crotch and realize that this woman is actually interested in controlling what's going on down there. And not just mine, but on a global scale. She's trying to reach out and not touch somebody. And there are *millions* like her.

I interview tons of people from church groups and hundreds of missionaries, ministers, rabbis, gospel singers, and theology students. They all seem like they're having a great time in life and at the show, but I'd rather keep my thingy to myself.

## You Ain't Nothin' but a Contestant

A short man named Travis is tucked away humbly into the line of interviewees. You'd never really notice him until you realize that he's wearing an Elvis-like outfit. Dear God, this guy thinks he looks like Elvis. He's about five foot two, in his late sixties, and looks as much like Elvis as I look like Britney Spears. But he is wearing all black, with studded oversize lapels, and has the Elvis hair and attitude. When I speak to him, I'm expecting to get a modicum of Elvis from his voice. Instead what I get is a weak nasal warble sounding a lot like a sick otter. I never pick people as contestants based on the costumes that they wear, and this guy is no exception, but he's a hoot to behold.

"Hey folks, Elvis is in the building!" I say, trying to humor him. "Welcome to the show, Travis."

"Glad to be here, baby," he says in a pathetic impression of the King.

"What do you do, Travis?"

"I'm an Elvis impersonator in Las Vegas," he weakly responds in a voice barely detectable even by radar.

"That's fascinating, Travis. And you make a living at it?"

"Not a good one, but I try."

"How did you get started doing this?" I ask with complete curiosity.

"Well, I've always thought that Elvis was the best performer in history, and this is how I honor the King. Been doing it for forty years. The sixties were the best, baby."

I have to assume that this guy probably did a slightly better impression of Elvis back in the sixties, and just never acknowledged the fact that he outgrew his ability. My guess is he was never very good at it even back then, but he's a great example of one of the deluded masses who can't let go of his prime.

## The Good Old Days

We often get large groups of senior citizens visiting the show. Most of them are well into their seventies, many into their eighties, and a few into their nineties. All in all, they seem to be having a good time in their retirement. I always ask them if they're having fun in life, and I usually get a resounding "Yes!" There's an occasional "Not really," and I always feel bad for them. But what the heck am I supposed to say to someone, "Gee, Gertrude, I'm sorry that your grandson is in prison and you've got gout"?

Nevertheless, no matter what they're feeling now, you just know that they all had a great time in their youths at one point or another. That may be hard for young people to imagine, but what's even harder to picture is that a lot of them were probably hot and sexy. Sort of like my next interviewee, Ruthie.

"Ruthie's here! Hi, Ruthie!"

"Hello," she responds conservatively.

"What do you spend your days doing, Ruthie?"

"Well, I like to dance, and crochet, and play bingo. Other than that, a whole lotta *nothin'*!"

"That sounds like a good life to me!"

"Well, it's a lot better than the life I used to have," she responds as she begins to loosen up a bit.

"And what life would that have been?" I ask curiously.

"I used to be a chorus girl for the Ziegfeld Follies. Damn near worked me to death!"

"Wow, that's amazing, Ruthie! What a great career!"

"Yeah, I know, it's hard to look at this old decrepit body and imagine that I was once cute."

"Not at all. I think you're still cute!"

"Well, thank you. You need your eyes examined."

## Walk-Through Divorce Court

I'm rarely thrown for a loop, but this interview stopped me in my tracks for the first time.

"Where are you from, Sy?" I say to this friendly, boyish young man in front of me.

"Newton, Massachusetts."

"And what do you do, Sy?"

"I'm a lawyer."

"Did you pass the bar the first time?" I quickly ask.

"Yeah," he swiftly responds.

"Would you tell me if you didn't?"

"Nope."

"Yes, folks!" I announce to the rest, "The man truly *is* a lawyer! Or should I say *liar*?" I add with a chuckle.

I often use this line on lawyers because it gets a laugh. But the ensuing conversation suddenly took a hard, screeching turn that would have thrown even a Nascar driver.

Standing next to Sy was his wife, Emma. She quickly commented on what I had just said.

"He *is* a damn liar," she murmurs under her breath.

"What was that, Emma?"

"I said he's a liar," she repeats with her arms tightly crossed.

"Why is that?" I ask.

" 'Cause he slept with my cousin and kept it from me up until a couple of minutes ago."

At first I think she's joking. But judging from the look on her face and her tone, I'm not sure.

"Wait a minute, Sy," I blurt, trying to make humor of it all. "Did you really sleep with her cousin?"

"Well, sorta," he shyly says.

"Okay, Sy, and why the hell would you be telling your wife on the line at *The Price Is Right* that you slept with her cousin?"

"'Cause he's a damn liar *and* an idiot," Emma quickly interjects.

"Oh my God, Sy, you guys are serious! This has got to be totally humiliating for you! And in front of all these other people!"

I just realize that I've gotten myself into a conversation that can't be easily backed out of without some sympathy, so I just say, "Things are going to be okay, you two. Just take it easy and you'll be okay."

I was so shocked at the awkwardness of this moment that I lost complete focus on the next couple of people. Remember, there were ten other people standing right there listening to this train wreck. Trying to gloss over the breakup of a marriage at a happy game-show interview was something for which no one could be prepared. I also wondered for a brief moment whether or not it was all an act to get attention. Was I being played, as had happened on occasion in the past? My intuition said no. Nevertheless, as I was interviewing the next couple of people, I saw out of the corner of my eye Emma mouthing to Sy with tight-lipped hostility, "You son of a bitch." My guess is that it was all real. As they walked away, she wouldn't get near him, and that was no act. If it was, it was an award-winning performance. As far as I was concerned, the curtain had dropped and the play was over. And, I suspect, so was their marriage.

# 12

# WE'LL FIT YOU TO A TEE

## The Great Shirts of
## *The Price Is Right*

**PRICE IS RIGHT** contestants have the best sense of humor of anyone on earth. And nowhere is their wit more apparent than in the T-shirts that they wear when they show up to a taping. These people spend ages planning, designing, and making these highly specialized, can't-wear-them-anywhere-else-on-earth shirts. Some are simple, some are silly, some tell a story, and some are even poignant.

No matter what, though, they're all creative, and they all want attention to be drawn to them. I'm sorry to say that, in spite of how great all these shirts are, it never, and I mean *never* influences my decision to choose them as a contestant. A good contestant is a good contestant, regardless of what they're wearing. If you're enthusiastic and fun, you could be wearing a burlap sack, and you'd have a good chance of being chosen. And just a reminder to those of you who started to make your way to the costume store. We don't allow costumes of any kind on the show. (Probably not even a burlap sack, actually.) We didn't want to go the way of *Let's Make a Deal* where the more outrageous you looked, the better (although I'm not all that convinced that they weren't more interested in great people over costumes either).

It does make the show fun, and Bob does acknowledge shirts sometimes when the person gets onstage. Not necessarily for its cleverness, but more for its content, like the older couple that has "Married sixty years" written on their shirts. That makes for good conversation onstage, but again, it didn't get anyone up there. It just happened to be a fun thing for Bob to notice. I've had people say to me, "We wanted to wear

*This group decided to pay homage to a birthday girl turning fifty by saying, "Wow, she's old." Very cold, guys, very cold.*

a shirt that said 'Ohio' on it, because you always pick people from Ohio . . . and we're from New Jersey!" The honest truth is, I am not having any torrid love affair with Ohio, and I'm not aware that more Ohioans get on than people from other states. Of course, if you're a ninety-five-year-old lady from Ohio who tells me she's going to seduce Bob if she wins a car because he's hot hot hot, then the Ohioans have it!

Here are some of the greatest hits in T-shirts that I've come across recently. Fashion police, get out your citations!

*These guys have their priorities well in order. No great pop singers for them. Bob is their American Idol.*

*This happy couple decided to dump their plans for an exotic getaway and spend their honeymoon at our show. Win a room, guys.*

*This guy conceived his kid in front of the TV while watching* The Price Is Right *and decided to name his kid after us. Thank God he wasn't doing it during* Jeopardy!

*Tonja proudly stood up and told me that Bob donated thousands of dollars to the organization that made her brain surgery possible.*

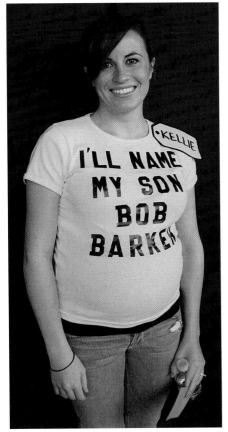

*This pregnant woman said she would dedicate her child to Bob, if only she got her way and won some "Plinko" cash. Is that all we are to you? A dollar sign? Oh wait, that is what we are.*

*Cyreeta made it up on stage, but not before letting us know how hot she thought Bob was.*

*This guy took some drastic measures to push the spay and neuter plug. Ouch.*

*Mary took a famous credit card commercial slogan and made a fun shirt out of it.*

*The ultimate optimists. These three decided to Photoshop themselves into the show whether they got on or not.*

**110**

Jeremy got onstage and won a car. He made
it clear where his educational priorities were
while attending UCSB.

Some people make lists of their goals.
Then there are those people who include
us on those lists of their goals.

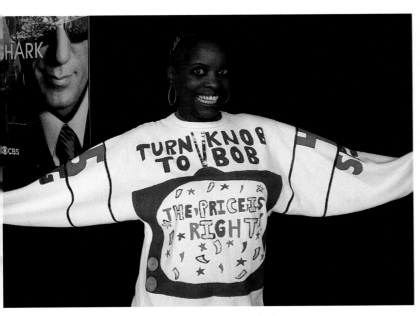

Rosiland tunes in to our show by twisting
knobs on her shirt.

Minnie Pearl has nothing on this lady.
She's got price tags all over her.

Andrew used his home state's letters to work in his birthday wish. Subtle.

Brittany ditched dance class to come here. Watch for a really bad pirouette in a couple of years when you're attending the ballet.

Ara brought his girlfriend, Ashley, out here from Wisconsin when they first started dating to show her around Hollywood. She saw CBS and said, "Oh my God! That's where they do *The Price Is Right!* I'd love to win a scooter." When he finally decided to pop the question, he got her tickets, put them into an envelope, gave her the envelope, and asked her to marry him.

Nicole believes that Bob is as tasty as bubble gum.

Marlene fashioned her birthday sentiment after our game "Flip Flop" by pointing out that she had to be 61 because, obviously, she wasn't 16.

Bob's famous Happy Gilmore line will live on for eternity.

If only we'd have had male models . . .

Gregg's wife gave him an ultimatum.

The front of these shirts seem innocent enough. I thought they were promising not to hurt Bob. It turns out that they had other plans for him.

Jason made it clear that breakfast just wouldn't be the same without his favorite meal . . . a steady diet of Bob.

I'm sure Bob is also grateful his parents weren't neutered, but he would be equally grateful for the word "neutered" to be spelled correctly.

115

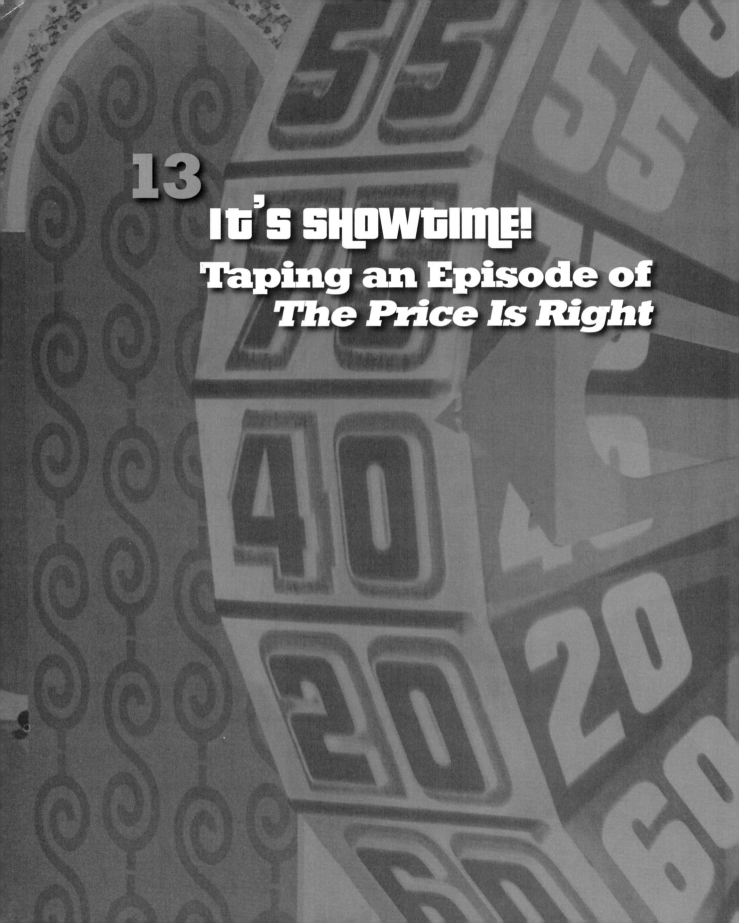

# 13

# IT'S SHOWTIME!
## Taping an Episode of *The Price Is Right*

**LIGHTS! CAMERA! PANIC!** When all the paperwork is in place, when the models' lips and stainless steel stoves glisten and every splotch of paint on primped cheek and pressed plywood awaits adulation, when Bob is dressed to the nines, and nine unknowing contenders in a sea of devotees await having their names called, the moment of truth is upon us. Most assuredly all hearts are a-poundin'. It's an exhilarating time. It's showtime.

Everyone is anxiously perched in his or her place minutes before the show. While announcer Rich Fields is getting the audience revved up, the booth, which is located up behind those rainbow-colored drapes you see in the back of the audience, is filled with staff sitting patiently until the clock strikes the precise minute that the show is supposed to start. We're usually right on schedule, if not ahead of it.

*The booth is the nerve center of the show during taping and resembles a NASA shuttle launch control room.*

Up in that booth sits Bart Eskander, the director, who will call all the shots, the traffic cop, as it were, who will tell everyone what to do and where to go. Next to him sits the assistant director, Fred Witten, who keeps time with a menagerie of stopwatches, making sure we actually have a one-hour show on tape when it's all done. Along with Bart, he communicates with the stage managers who will subsequently tell Bob

if he's under or over the allotted time. He also prepares the cameramen for upcoming shots via headsets and microphones. The technical director, Dave Hallmark, is ready and rarin' to push all the buttons and slide all the levers on his high-tech switchboard-a-tron-o-matic thing that creates all those fun video effects you see at home, like the flipping of a scene, or the "peeling back" of a corner on one shot to reveal another shot.

Our production coordinator, Karen, has all the prices in front of her, and during the show she'll yell out whether it's a win or a loss at any given time so that the director can anticipate what a contestant is going to do. After all, if someone wins a forty-thousand-dollar car, don't you think there's a good chance that he or she might go berserk and jump all over the stage? If that happens, the director will want to communicate that to the camera people and say something like, "Watch out, Marty. This lady's going to find out in a second that she's won and she's gonna go crazy. Stay with her." It's a little edge that helps everyone prepare for every possible moment.

Our executive in charge of production, Sue, sits behind all these people and keeps records of outstanding moments in the show as well as having an overall eagle's watch of the show. If there are problems, she'll be all over it.

The lighting director is ready to bring up all the specific lights from the booth, and the video operator is tweaking his knobs and buttons to make sure all the colors and contrast are correct with all the cameras.

The woman who gives us all those electronically generated characters, like the product names that flash up on the screen, as well as the final credits, is up there typing away with her special electronic graphics keyboard.

I'm up in a separate booth adjacent to the director's booth. I sit with an audio engineer, Maryann Jorgenson, who actually plays back all the music digitally from a special computer, and every music cue is loaded and ready to go. I'll eventually cue her at various points to lay in all that music as we're actually shooting the show.

The "sweetener," Angee Gates, is ready to augment the applause, and add "oooohs" and "aaaaahs" if needed. She's got a device that's a sort of modified musical keyboard that musicians use, but her keys don't activate musical notes. They activate audience sounds, which are occasionally needed when the audience's energy dies off on us. The spot in the show that will need it most is after the last contestant gets called down and the other three hundred-some-odd people realize they're not coming on down. It's somewhat reflected in their level of enthusiasm, so until we can get them a bit hyped up again, our sweetener fills in the gaps with some canned applause and cheers.

*The audio mixer and music technician poised for beautiful noise.*

The audio mixer, David Vaughn, is up in that booth, too,

and is also ready for the wall of sound that is about to arise. Remember, every element of the sound you hear comes through this guy's console as we're taping, so his hands are spread out over the thousands of buttons like an ice skating rink organist.

There's always a bit of jittery anticipation that goes on in my tummy right before we start. After all, there are tons of unanswered questions in my mind. Will the computer that controls the music work okay? Will the contestants be good, or will they totally tank? Will global warming ruin my daffodils?

It's time. Holy heart attack, Batman, it's time. The moment when all the work of the past six weeks actually pays off and comes together into one big exhilarating rush of showbiz satisfaction. This is why I got into the business. My father was right. There really isn't a boring day in show business. Here we go.

The clock strikes, and the countdown begins.

"Five, four, three, two, one," counts the assistant director, like the blastoff of a rocket. At that moment, all hell breaks loose.

The director calls, "Up on camera three," as we fade up from a black screen and are greeted, no, accosted by the vision of a hysterical audience going wild as the camera pans across everyone's faces. The cheering and screaming is so loud that it makes the eardrums vibrate at a deafening level.

"Cue, Rich!" the director shouts, as Rich calls down the first contestant.

"Mary Griswald, come on down!" Rich hollers.

"Announce!" the director orders again, as the second frenzied contestant runs on down.

In the meantime, Bob is backstage quietly standing behind door 2, practically pressed up against the back of it, ready to make his entrance. He is able to see the first four contestants come on down with a little TV monitor that is perched up on the side of the big door.

"You are the first four contestants on . . . *The Price Is Right*!" Rich announces. "And here is the star of *The Price Is Right*, Bob Barker!"

A stagehand manually tugs on a rope, sort of like one might open a drape, but instead, this rope controls the wooden panels in door 2 that slide open, just wide enough to let Bob through the big door.

Out he bounds with a big smile on his face, smoothly gliding across that big stage with panache. The audience goes wild. They leap to their feet and cheer. The sound reaches levels beyond a twenty-thousand-seat stadium, a cheer that rivals that of a mob having just seen an amazing home run at a baseball game. After the model hands Bob his famous long-stemmed, wired microphone, he bows and greets his audience with a warm welcome.

The audience is aglow with joy. The fervent applause increases as hoots, cheers, and hollers come from every single audience member. They each applaud with such vigor, standing at tallest attention and applauding as if each clap is paying tribute to his accomplishments. Bob immediately tosses the attention over to the first item up for bid.

Back to the booth. The director says, "Turn the turntable, take camera two, and announce!" The stage manager hears this through his headset and cues a stagehand to push the button that activates the turntable.

"It's a new stereo system!"

After the contestants have seen the prize and they're busy bidding, no time is wasted behind the turntable. The turntable and prize rotate back. A group of stagehands immediately roll up a platform to lift off the prize and take it away. They quickly and quietly load up the next thing needed for that position, perhaps a game that will be played at some point in the show.

The hallway behind the studio is ablaze with worker-bee-like people rushing to get things set. So much is happening at once that, if backstage, it's easy to forget there's actually a show going on in front of the doors. But we're painfully reminded of that as the stage manager yells at the stagehand, "Hey, Joe! Get out of the big door! I'm about to open it!" Joe, or Sam, or whoever, usually gets out in time, sometimes right in sync with the actual door movement. Sometimes Joe doesn't make it in time, and his butt gets seen on national television.

"What the hell happened there?" the director shrieks. "Get that stagehand out of there!"

Bob continues. By this time the contestant is finishing up her game. There's a win!

The contestant is all over the stage because she's just won a cruise.

"Take four! Take two! Keep up with her, guys!" the director says.

"We'll be right back with more pricing games after this," Bob says as we go to commercial.

"Fly it in!" the stage manager shouts, and the flyman, the guy who drops stuff with cables and counterweights, quickly heaves on the thick steel cable that brings things in and out. A huge canvas soars in from the rafters above, and if you're not careful, you'll get bonked by it. It shields the audience from what is coming up next. Don't want to ruin any surprises. The doors open to evacuate the game that was just played and, like two ships that pass in the night, they roll in the next game, or if it's after act three, the big wheel. A dozen people scurry in and lay carpet down. The electric department, seemingly out of nowhere, pulls wires the size of the transatlantic phone cables and connects the electronics on the game.

"Who has a question?" Bob queries the audience, as this other mayhem is going on behind that big canvas drop.

"I do!" an anxious audience member responds.

In the booth, the word is given by the stage manager that we're ready to go go go!

"Let's roll!" says the director.

"Five, four, three, two, one . . . and we're up on four!"

"Rich, who's our next contestant?" Bob says.

"Well, Bob, it's . . ."

Disaster has struck backstage. As the next contestant does his thing, there has been a massive traffic jam in the hallway. They have only minutes, or seconds, to unsnarl it or we'll have to stop tape, and that is not really an option to be considered if not necessary. Not only that, but it seems that the next game we're supposed to play had gotten caught on something earlier, and a light on the game has been busted.

"Damn," barks the head grip. "Tell the booth we've got a busted game!" he says to a fellow stagehand.

*Bob fields questions from curious audience members during a commercial break.*

A crew guy runs to the stage manager and tells him that there's a broken game. He, in turn, tells the director through his headset.

"Can it be played without the light?" asks the director through his headset microphone.

"I think so. We need to tell the producer and Barker," responds the stage manager. The stage manager tells the producer onstage, who will ultimately tell Bob if he thinks there is looming doom ahead. While the products are being announced by Rich, the producer, or sometimes the stage manager, sneaks up to Bob and tells him of the impending problem. Bob assures that he'll handle it.

Bob handles it beautifully. He may even make a comment on

*Bob has a built-in clock in his head and brings the show in on time right down to the minute every single day.*

the malfunction on air, make a joke about it, and go ahead with the game by moving a graphic or set piece by hand, or just saying, "You're a winner!"

As the game is played, there are cues from our other production coordinator, Gina, right there onstage: Thumbs up if a win, thumbs down if a loss, which will tell the sound effects person who sits behind her to hit the win bell or a loss buzzer. The sound effects console, just like the sweetener's console, is full of activity during all this. Honks, dings, whoops, buzzes . . . all essential to the production, all extremely purposeful, like an elevator arrival ding or a car horn before a potential accident. Each communicates an idea and either prevents something or enhances something.

This is just like live television. Or at least, we treat it as such. We all get it into our heads from the onset as production people that "The show must go on" and that we cannot get lazy by assuming things will get fixed later, or that a stop won't kill us. It's easy to do that in television and film, as most shows take endless amounts of time to stop and do things over again and again until it's just right. Not on our show. Part of the charm and energy comes from the screw-up factor. The audience actually enjoys it tremendously when a mistake is acknowledged and dealt with on the air. It's as if they've been let in on some kind of secret, and only they get to know it. Bob even jokes about it sometimes off camera. He'll occasionally say after a goof-up, "Don't tell anyone this happened when you get home."

The hour goes by quickly. The second wheel spinning is there before you know it.

"Spin the wheel, Gladys," Bob says to the current contestant. Beep beep beep beep beep beep beep. "You've got seventy cents. Are you going to spin again or stay?"

Rolling, shifting, connecting, adjusting, placing, pushing, dragging. The crew has already started to set the showcases. Quickly and qui-

*The backstage hustle resembles a fire drill during the show.*

etly, all the large set pieces and prizes need to be brought in and placed as the show continues on camera.

In the meantime, the dressing rooms are abuzz with combs, curling irons, dresses, and costumes flying everywhere. No sense of panic really. Just a steady, focused German train-like timeliness and dedication to get things done pronto. That can be a real challenge when I've asked the makeup artist to make a model look like she's tired, or the time I wanted a constant worried look on a model's face. It required her to blank out her eyebrows

*Lanisha is surrounded by all the tools of beauty.*

with a special skin-colored gum, and paint new ones on her with a furrowed brow. And all in a matter of minutes.

There's so little time, the wigs get plunked down on models' heads like a cap gets popped onto a jar in an assembly line, followed by hair getting curled or ratted, or whatever is needed for the character.

"Everyone in your places! One minute!" bellows the stage manager.

"Just a second. I need hairspray," states the model.

"You're fine! Let's go!"

All the models shuffle quickly across the stage in their spike heels, or duck feet, or roller skates if necessary. Today the showcase is a sketch called "The Diver." I wanted to do a scene that looked like it was underwater, and prizes would float down to the model. The rigging was clever, and the crew worked fast to get the effect done quickly during the short break.

"Five, four, three, two, one," says one of the other stage managers. He waves his hand to Bob, indicating that we're on the air.

Bob is on, and explains to the two top contestants at the showcase podia, "Mary, you're the top winner, and, Josh, you're the runner-up. Each of you will be shown a showcase of fine prizes, and, Mary, you may bid on your showcase or pass."

Hopefully by the time we hear those words, everything is in its place. No room for preening or repositioning anymore. Bob tosses it to Rich, and the showcase begins.

"Take four, open door two, announce!" says the director.

*Diligently setting up an "underwater" scene during a commercial break is a testament to good planning.*

Rich announces. "Your showcase takes place underwater, as our diver discovers some interesting things under the bay."

The first thing they bring in is a DVD player that is being held on very fine fishing line, suspended from a long pole and dropped from a very tall ladder by our special effects crew. Next the flyman slowly drops in a big motorcycle. And finally they roll in a car that is being driven by none other than a model wearing a fish head. I asked the technical director to make the video wavy, sort of like water, to add to the effect of being under a bay. As a little joke of mine, the sketch ended with the diver putting a "For Sale" sign on the car and selling it on . . . what else? . . . e-Bay. Don't hit me. I know it was a stupid joke, but I thrive on stupid jokes. The showcase went on without a hitch, and looked great on the air.

"Mary, do you want to bid or pass?" Bob asks.

*The special effects looked terrific on the air, and most important, no hairdos were ruined in the making of this underwater showcase.*

"I'll pass it to Josh."

"Josh, what do you bid on that showcase?"

The big doors at this point have been closed, and the models have run backstage to get ready for the second showcase. Stagehands have moved some of the diver stuff off the stage in a matter of moments.

As soon as Josh bids, Bob says, "Mary, this is your showcase."

"Take four, open door three, announce!" commands the director.

The door opens to reveal a living room. Rich reads the copy.

More directions: "Roll it on!"

They roll on a new snowmobile in front of the living room.

"Fly it in! Take three!"

They fly in a wall to reveal a cruise to the Caribbean.

"And this showcase can be yours if the price is right," concludes the announcer.

The second contestant bids, and we go to a commercial.

At this point, we're all told by our production coordinator, "Second showcase won." The director tells the stage manager which showcase won because, at the end of the show, the winner will be running out to the doors to stand next to the prizes that she won. We need to know what to have out there so we don't end up showing the winner things that she didn't win. In a matter of seconds, everything is in place, and we're ready to reveal the winner.

The winner is revealed, Bob thanks the loser, and after he has done his famous "Help control the pet population, have your pet spayed or neutered" plug, they all go out onstage, along with their loved ones who have bounded up onstage to wave good-bye on national television as the credits roll by. Fade to black.

A sigh of relief is breathed by all. It always feels like we just ran a very short but intense marathon. The breath-catching moments right at the end are truly satisfying, assuming you didn't mess up too badly in one area or another.

As soon as we're finished, the director announces to everyone, "Take a break for twenty minutes. We start rehearsing at three twenty on the dot!"

Everyone scurries away, the audience files out, and amazingly, the stage is dark and silent within seconds. What was just abuzz with activity is now a serene, lifeless place. It's hard to imagine that only moments before, this stage was filled with seeming chaos.

Everyone readjusts their thinking as they scamper off and get themselves into rehearsal mode, and twenty minutes later, we start the whole rehearsal thing all over again for the next show, which will be in a couple of hours.

I, in the meantime, have run down to the winning contestants backstage to thank

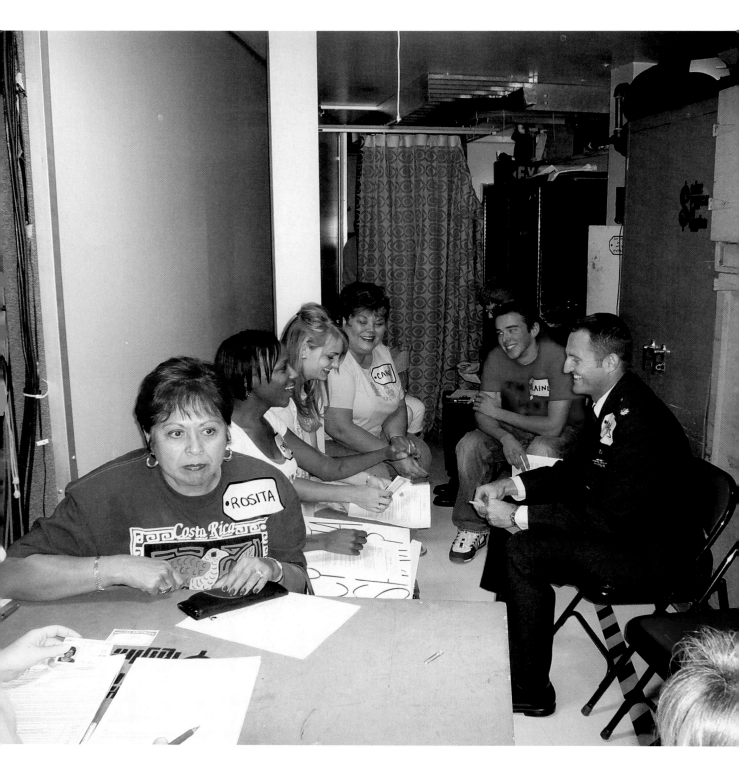

*The "checking out" of contestants after the show is an exciting if not sobering experience.*

them for being on the show. They are filling in forms with the prize department and usually have one of two looks on their faces: either a look of total befuddled excitement and disbelief or a glazed-over spaciness that is a result of not really knowing how to react to what's just happened to them. This is also a somewhat sobering moment for them, as this is when they are informed that they're responsible for paying the taxes on all this loot. It's essentially added to their income at the end of the year. Do I hear the hair follicles of accountants across the land standing on end?

The reality also sets in that they have just won a giant popcorn machine, and thoughts of "Where the hell am I going to put this thing?" dance across their bemused little mugs. Occasionally they'll forfeit the prize but usually they're so grateful that they figure out some way to deal with it.

After a mountain of paperwork and contact numbers are given to them, they walk off into the crowd and often get cheers from fellow onlookers outside who either just attended the show, or people who are awaiting the same experience out on the line for the next show.

It's as if they're a celebrity taking a walk of fame, virtual flashbulbs going off on the imaginary red carpet, glorious admiration and envy abound. It's a great reminder to all those in line for the next show that, yes indeed, people really do win things on this show. Yes, you can really get tons of free stuff and be a star for a few minutes, or even a few weeks if you figure out a way to milk it long enough!

# 14

# COME ON DOWN!

## Let's Talk to the Winners

**what could be better** than hearing your own name followed by those illustrious words "Come on down!"? Even if you're not a fan of the show, you'd be stoked beyond belief if you had the chance to have this much fun, be on television, and walk away with a new car, new silverware, or a free trip to Italy.

The residual effects of appearing on the show are more than you'll realize, too. While your hibachi may grow rusty and ashen, you will still be talking about your experience on *The Price Is Right* until the day you die. And the attention you'll get from your local newspaper or merely your neighbors, friends, and family will give you a taste of celebrity that few experience in life. And you'll have it on DVD for generations to come. Show it to your grandchildren so you can say, "See how cute Grandma used to be back in those days?"

I'm sharing with you some of my favorite winners on the show. Not all walked away with 401K-size winnings, but they all had a blast, and all came home with a smile the size of a crescent moon. Some indeed did make a killing, but before they did, they had a nice chat and experienced "The Stanish Inquisition."

## Dale

The family I was about to interview seemed to have a natural comic response to my questions. I asked a young man in the group where he was from and he responded, "From number forty-nine." When I asked someone else why they were here, she answered, "Number forty-nine." Yet another said, "Forty-nine drove me here." Then the husband said, "I'm with forty-nine." At this point, I was dying to meet number forty-nine. And there she was, wearing the number 49 under her nametag.

Dale, the notorious number forty-nine, was a feisty sixty-year-old blond woman with a great southern accent. She had as much character as her family did, with a sharp voice to match her wit, and a truly animated face.

STAN: There's Dale, the famous number forty-nine!
DALE: I'm sixty years young today! It's my birthday!

STAN: Where are you from?

DALE: We flew all the way out here from Birmingham, Alabama. And because I'm out here for my sixtieth birthday, I've got to win two showcases. My mother was on the show twenty-five years ago, and she lost everything . . . didn't win a penny, and I've got to redeem the family honor.

STAN: You've got some high hopes there, darlin'. You know you have to be within two hundred fifty dollars to win both showcases.

DALE: I do. I know that, but I'm good.

Dale was a shoo-in. I was so taken with her delightful laugh and joyful expression that I was excited to see how she'd perform on the show.

She came on down, and didn't disappoint. Tons of energy and sheer elation made it all the more fun to watch her. Because her shirt said it was her sixtieth birthday, Bob said, "It's Dale's sixtieth birthday, and I just happened to have a lovely little birthday present," at which moment Dale interrupted and said, "I hope it's big." Bob, stopped in his tracks, looked at the audience in his best dry Jack Benny style, and said, "Some women are never satisfied with *anything*!" It got a big laugh from the audience. He then continued, "But I bet you'll be satisfied with *that*!" which was followed by the announcer saying, "It's a new van!"

Dale played a game called "Cover Up" and after several strategic moves, her winning

eventually depended on one correct number. She waited anxiously for Bob to tell her whether that last number was correct or not. When Bob asked, "Is she a winner?" Dale said, "*Pleeeease!*" To which Bob jokingly replied, "I can't stand it when contestants beg. Don't beg. Take it like a sixty-year-old woman." Sure enough, Dale won the van, in addition to a treadmill, which she won to get up onstage.

**Fast Forward** A couple of months after her appearance, I happened to talk to her the day after she took delivery of her new car.

She was thrilled, and said that her Dodge Caravan had her name on the sticker, "Made especially for Dale."

She also had a great story that she was reluctant to tell about her visit to the show. I got it out of her though.

> DALE: When I came to the show, I had a birthday shirt and a birthday hat on. I got there at five in the morning, and it wasn't a good hair day. I took my hat off and I thought *Oh my God, if I get called down there, I can't go down with hat hair!* So we went to the Kmart right across the street, and we went in to get a curling iron and an adapter so we could plug it into the cigarette lighter, so there I was in the parking lot doin' my hair. It didn't come out very good, but it was better than hat hair.
>
> STAN: How did your family react when you told them you won on *The Price Is Right*?
>
> DALE: Nobody believed me. I called them and said, "Guess what? We just got on *The Price Is Right* and we won a car," and they said, "Yeah, right." I had to beg and plead for them to believe me. And then of course they went crazy. My son was on the phone for hours and hours. He even put me on the phone and made me talk to people I never heard of.
>
> STAN: How does it feel to get called on down?
>
> DALE: I was very nervous. It's almost surreal, like you don't know what you're doing. Like you're in another world. It's very loud, and you're in a daze.
>
> STAN: How was it to see yourself on television?
>
> DALE: Well, it was like *Is that me up there?* That TV will put weight on your butt, ya know.

## Colleen

**C**olleen, a totally stoked, bouncy, sandy blond forty-eight-year-old from Alpine, Utah, was ready and rarin' to go for this interview. Before I got to her, Gary, her husband, wanted to let me know that all he does is her Honey-do list.

> STAN: So, Colleen, he's calling you high-maintenance.
> COLLEEN: I am! (She lets out a shriek and howl.)
> STAN: What do you do when you're not pushing your husband around?
> COLLEEN: I'm a substitute teacher at Lone Peak High School.
> STAN: You get any respect?
> COLLEEN: I get it all!

At that point, Colleen was shaking, laughing, shouting, almost out of control of her emotions. Her voice could have been heard in Tibet.

> STAN: Had too much Red Bull today, Colleen?
> COLLEEN: No!
> STAN: Too much Starbucks?
> COLLEEN: No!
> STAN: You always this happy?
> COLLEEN: I'm always this happy (crazed scream) . . . You didn't ask
>       me where I was from.
> STAN: I assumed you were from the same place as everyone else in
>       your group.
> COLLEEN: Well, I wanted to say I'm from heaven!

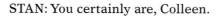

> STAN: You certainly are, Colleen.

It truly was Colleen's day, and she was about to enter her own little "heaven."

Her enthusiasm was infectious, and it showed every minute. She won a large wine cooler in her one bid, and when she ran up onstage, she sort of, shall I say, accosted Bob from behind. "Oh! I'm being attacked . . . I'm being mugged on my own show!" Bob said as she grabbed his shoulders and jumped around behind him, mouth wide open and pointing to him in large gestures as if to say, *Hey guys, this is Bob Barker! I'm here with Bob Barker!* She played a game called "One Wrong Price," and unfortunately lost the game, but she *did* spin a dollar on the wheel, which got her a thousand bucks and a shot at the showcase. Indeed, she also ended up winning her showcase, and raked in a cell phone, a Rolex watch, and a Pontiac Grand Prix.

**Fast Forward** When I spoke to her some months later, she was just as fun and enthusiastic (without the screaming) as she was the day I met her.

> COLLEEN: I've been milking this
>     for the last two months. We show the tape every day at the high school.
> STAN: How did everyone react to your winning on the show?
> COLLEEN: Everyone said, "You're lying, you're pulling our leg. No no."
>     Then everyone called me a celebrity. At school everyone would say,
>     "Oh, you're the *Price Is Right* lady."
> STAN: How did you feel when you heard your name to come on down?
> COLLEEN: My biggest fear is that I have a weak bladder, and when I
>     jumped up, you get that urge, you know, and you think *Oh my God!* And
>     so, as I go to grab my crotch, I thought *There's a camera on me. Don't
>     grab your crotch!* And I had to consciously tell myself *Don't grab your
>     crotch!* When I got up onstage, and I spun the dollar on the big wheel, I
>     thought again *Don't grab your crotch, don't grab your crotch.*
> STAN: Anything negative happen out of an experience like this? For in-
>     stance, people wanting something from you now that you're a big
>     winner.
> COLLEEN: I have four older sisters, and it's like having four mothers. They
>     kept telling me how to spend the money, what I can and what I can't
>     do. I said I'd probably sell the watch, and they told me, "Well then you
>     better pay off your credit cards." I sold the watch (my neighbor said,
>     "I'm interested"). My nephew called me about the wine cooler because
>     we don't drink wine. He said, "Hey, what are you going to do about the

wine cooler?" and I said, "Oh, I don't know. Maybe we'll have to start drinking." He said, "My parents really want it, so can I buy it off you?"

STAN: How did you like seeing yourself on TV?

COLLEEN: You know how they say that TV adds ten pounds. No, it added fifty! I had a wedgie. When I turned around, it was just awful. But I guess after you stand outside for nine hours, ugh . . . your hair is flat. You know.

I was happy to know that Colleen had such a great time as a result of being on the show. I also felt a little bad that she had to discover her backside on national television. Call me crazy, but I'm thinking a wedgie is a good trade-off for a Pontiac.

## Bradley

Just like Colleen, Brad appeared overcaffeinated too. He was a twenty-year-old hyper guy visiting with a group of fraternity brothers. I noticed that he had a scar on his face. I decided not to ask what happened, but boy, did I get a story anyway . . . in the form of the world's longest run-on sentence. (Read this really really fast, and that's how he told this story.)

STAN: Hey, Brad! Where are you from?

BRAD: I'm from Phoenix, Arizona, and I'm a psychology major, but, Stan, I really want to tell you the story behind these scars on my face.

STAN: Ten words or less, Brad.

BRAD: I've been getting crazy with this fraternity getting this *Price Is Right* thing settled. I'm the man in charge, trying to get it all done . . . I know, it was supposed to be ten

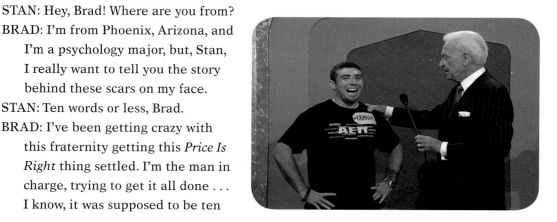

words or less . . . just a couple of days ago, someone came up to me and told me that *The Price Is Right* sucked, one of my fraternity brothers jokin' around, I gave him a little shove, you know, just kidding around, and he gave me a little shove back, and I tripped over my foot and scraped my face on the concrete defending the honor of *The Price Is Right.*

Being a pull-the-string chatty doll doesn't always work for everyone when trying out for the show, but in this case, it paid off for Brad. He was just so charming and sincere.

When Brad made it up onstage, Bob noted the scar on his forehead. Brad told the story he told me during the interview, and said, "I got this defending *The Price Is Right,* and defending you, Bob." The audience burst into applause, and Bob, being impressed with the determination and patriotism this kid had for the show, added, "I'm not at all worried about anyone else in the whole country ever being in a fight for that reason because there is undoubtedly no one else who will ever say that *The Price Is Right* sucks! . . . This young man deserves something *really* nice." And of course, it was . . . *a new car!*

Brad played "The Money Game," and when he won the Pontiac G6, he was clearly on a high . . . literally. He became airborne, as he jumped about as high as any contestant ever had, practically hitting the lights above. He was a great contestant, and as Bob always says, "A loyal friend, and true." At no other time has that been better demonstrated than by someone who gets into a fight about our show!

**Fast Forward** When we spoke months later, I really got a good sample of his jovial sense of humor.

> STAN: So how are you enjoying your prizes?
> BRAD: I got the car, but not the rug yet. I'm really depressed about the rug right now. Actually, they delivered the car to my house right on a truck.
> STAN: Were you preparing for your trip to the show ahead of time in any special way?
> BRAD: It was kind of crazy. The night before the show, I had an exam that

day, and I actually didn't go to sleep at all that night, studied for the exam the entire night, did my exam that afternoon. Then we stayed up that night, and drove that night. I was on zero sleep the entire time.

STAN: How did your friends and neighbors react when you got home?

BRAD: Everybody knew already. It was phenomenal. My mom lives in Australia. I don't get to see her that often, but she came in and she was there when we watched the show. There were twenty people crammed into my little fraternity room. My mom was laughing about how she thought my pants were going to fall down.

STAN: How do you think you look on TV?

BRAD: I thought I looked beautiful. I thought I looked like I was having the time of my life, and I recall having the time of my life.

STAN: How are you going to deal with the taxes you have to pay on the car?

BRAD: I have a very loving father. He was kind enough to front me the money I would need in order to pay the taxes.

STAN: Anything you'd like to say to close this?

BRAD: I would like to say, if I could, thank you, Matt, for pushing me over, and saying *The Price Is Right* sucked.

I appreciate Brad's tribute to his friend Matt. My advice, though, to all those who want to be on *The Price Is Right*: Don't perform any self-mutilation or acts of sacrificial violence to get yourself or your friends on the show. I prefer that contestants not be bloody or dismembered.

## Daveon

People often tell me that they spend an appreciable amount of time praying to win something on our show. Especially if they're theology students. There was a large group of them at the show one day. In the case of Daveon, who was a part of this enthusiastic group, his prayers came to fruition. An amazingly charismatic nineteen-year-old, Daveon exuded confidence and explained to me that his prayers had excellent timing.

DAVEON: I hail from sunny California . . . land of stahhhhhhhs!

STAN: Land of the stars, that's right. What do you spend your days doing?

DAVEON: I am a theological studies major and a (he sings) muuuuuuusic miiiiiiinor!

STAN: You going to sing for Bob later?

DAVEON: I definitely will. You tell Bob I'm here and I'll sing for him.

STAN: Or are you just going to preach at him?

DAVEON: I'll do both.

STAN: Great! I'd like to see you do both at the same time.

Daveon was remarkable on the show. Even Bob said, as Daveon ran up onstage, "Just from the way you left contestant's row and flew up those steps, you impress me. You are an energetic, excitable young man."

No question about that, but unfortunately he lost his game, "Pathfinders," in which he was playing for a car. But fate was on his side, and what was meant to be was meant to be, because he was given a second chance and he went on to spin the wheel, got a thousand dollars, and another five thousand in his bonus spin. He then won his show-case, which included free weights, a pool table, and a Buick Lucerne for a total of about $52,000. He was a really intense winner too . . . one of those guys who kind of became "possessed" (pardon the expression, Daveon) and did the inspirational-shaking-chicken-dance thing. At the end of the show, when his group joined him onstage, he dropped to his knees and looked toward the heavens, and even though we couldn't hear what he was saying during the closing credits, I *know* he was thanking God for his winnings. And when you hear what happened to him just a few days before, you'll understand why.

**Fast Forward** I called him on his cell phone a couple of months later, and guess where he was?

STAN: So, Daveon, have you gotten your prizes yet?

DAVEON: I'm actually driving one as we speak! It's a wonderful present!

STAN: What does it feel like to get a free car?

DAVEON: Well, I had come to *The Price Is Right* with the hope of winning a car. I had really been having a lot of car troubles. I was on the freeway and my engine just fell out. It was a ninety-five Mercury Tracer. I went to the car dealer the day before the show, and I spoke to my mom about getting a car, and she said, "I don't advise you on getting a new car. I'd prefer that you get a used car." So I

went to the dealer and looked at a car, and it wasn't exactly the greatest, so I was, like, I have to get to *The Price Is Right*. My school had been planning a trip to the show, but I got wait-listed. There were too many people and not enough seats. They [the group] said, "You might as well not even come. We don't want to get your hopes up and not be able to come." They told me to be there at eight o'clock, and I got there at seven thirty.

STAN: How long did it take for you to become a celebrity among your friends?

DAVEON: We had a bus from the school, and by the time I got back to the bus, there were already people texting me, congratulating me. I guess my friends had already been calling people.

STAN: How did your family react?

DAVEON: I told my mom on the phone about one prize at a time, and she was screaming so long, and I'd try to tell her, "Wait, Mom, I'm not finished." I had to calm her down because the neighbors were going to think there was something wrong and call the police. My grandmother kept telling me that I was making this up, so I had to let her speak to someone on the bus.

STAN: What was the first thing that went through your mind when you heard your name to come on down?

DAVEON: I was very excited, but at the time, I was trying to figure out *How am I going to do this? How am I going to get a new car?* I couldn't get out of my seat. There were a lot of people blocking me, so my friends kind of picked me up and tossed me into the aisle.

STAN: How did people at home react to you when they saw the show?

DAVEON: Everyone from my school, even people from my church, laughed at how I danced when I won.

STAN: What did you think about the way you looked on TV?

DAVEON: I looked like I was in my element. I said, "Is that how my head is shaped?" It showed me like I really am. There's nothing like seeing yourself on tape.

STAN: Anything you want to say about your amazingly good fortune in appearing on the show?

DAVEON: I think it was a divine setup. It was meant to happen. I actually lead a Bible study on campus, and I was talking to a friend about how I was wanting a car, a used car, and there's a scripture about God doing more than we expect. It's in Ephesians, chapter 3, verse 20. My friend said, "Why are you asking for a used car, when you should be asking for a new car?" I said I couldn't afford a new car.

STAN: Well, Daveon, you didn't have to. Congratulations!

**Vicky** The Biggest Winner in Daytime *Price Is Right* History

**V**icky (known as Vicki Ann on the show) was one of those people who opened up the minute I spoke to her. She was a vivacious woman in her fifties whose short blond hair and loads of enthusiasm made her a good choice for the show. What was about to happen to her was beyond any expectation she or anyone else could have had coming to a show like *The Price Is Right*.

STAN: Hey, Vicki Ann! Where are you from?

VICKY: I'm from Chicago, Illinois (Wheaton).

STAN: That's a good place to be from. What do you do?

VICKY: I'm a retired dentist.

STAN: No more spit and blood for you, eh, Vicki Ann?

VICKY: No more spit and blood . . . that's right. We're here for our twenty-sixth wedding anniversary.

STAN: How cool is that! Congrats!

VICKY: We also came out for our daughter's volleyball tournament. She plays for the University of Tennessee.

STAN: How can a dentist find time to watch *The Price Is Right*?"

VICKY: I've watched it for over thirty years.

STAN: What, you watched while you were drilling patients? Great!

VICKY: Yes, I watched it with my patients.

STAN: A lot of *screaming* patients, right? They must have loved you.

Vicky had this huge, amused grin during her entire appearance on the show. And grin she should have. As the biggest winner in our show's daytime history, she won a spa, a trip to New York, a camera, a home theater system, a video arcade game, a thou-

sand bucks on the wheel, and *three* cars, including a Saturn Sky, a Dodge Caravan, and an awesome Dodge Viper. A total of $147,517 was the booty. She won her game, called "Pushover," and won both showcases because, as the rules dictate, she bid within $250 of the actual retail price of her showcase. It doesn't happen a lot, but it sure happened that day for Vicky!

**Fast Forward** Obviously Vicky thoroughly enjoyed her experience (what's not to enjoy?) and like most others who go through this, felt that she had left her body during the entire thing. Vicky was an experienced teacher and lecturer, so she was no stranger to being in front of crowds. That may explain why she was pretty calm for most of her appearance on the show. It was also a bit of disbelief that kept her partially detached from the whole ordeal as it was happening.

STAN: Did you get all your cars yet?

VICKY: We got the Viper. We got that last week. We went to the dealership to pick it up and thought . . . okay! . . . It's a beautiful car. It's black with a silver stripe. It's in the garage, and every once in a while, we pull it out in the driveway. Then we put it back in the garage.

STAN: Not going to drive it that much, huh?

VICKY: I don't drive a stick shift! At first we thought we'd sell it, but we're growing attached to it.

STAN: What about the other cars?

VICKY: Since the production on that Saturn Sky is way backed up and they couldn't get it in a reasonable amount of time, they gave us the money instead.

STAN: And the other stuff?

VICKY: I talked to the hot tub people, and that was going to be delivered in December, but we had twelve inches of snow. The video arcade game . . . I enjoy playing it. I've never played with one before.

STAN: How did you initially decide to come to the show?

VICKY: Well, as I told you, I'm a dentist and I was a professor at Loyola dental school and at the University of Illinois, and I practiced with my dad on certain days. And whenever I would be practicing, there was a TV in the office in the reception room, and at ten o'clock, we'd have *The Price Is Right* on. Then I retired and I was at home more and had been watching it more. I said to my husband, "Why don't we go to *The Price Is Right* to watch the taping," and he's like, "I don't want to go and do that!" and I said, "Aw c'mon, I've always wanted to do this." My husband knew that you had to be in line a long time and said, "I don't want to be in line for eight hours!" And I said, "C'mon, how many times are you going to do this?" It was our twenty-sixth wedding anniversary, so how I finally got him to go was that I said, "For my anniversary present, you can come with me to *The Price Is Right*." That way he wouldn't complain and would be nice. He was also scared to death that he was going to be picked.

STAN: How did you tell the volleyball team and your family that you won?

VICKY: I didn't want to tell my daughter until we saw her in person. So the next morning at breakfast at the hotel, my husband took the little sign that they made for us that said "$147,000," and we go down to the restaurant and the Tennessee team is eating in the back room with the coaches, so my daughter said, "So, Dad, how was *The Price Is Right*? because she knew he didn't want to go. He said, "Your mom did really good." And so he holds up the sign. Now my husband is always joking around with my daughter, and he does this all the time. The teammates are all saying, "Really, Mr. Sadowski?" And my daughter is saying, "Don't believe him. He does this all the time. It's not true." Gradually as we're telling the other parents about this experience, the team is saying, "Mrs. Sadowski, you're not kidding, are you?" And my husband said, "No!" and he showed them the paperwork with the prizes on them, and my daughter said, "Dad, you had your secretary at work type these up." And he said, "No!" And she said, "Okay, what did she

win?" And he told her, "A Dodge Viper and a trip to New York and a Caravan . . ." and there was this one moment in time, about thirty minutes after we started all this, where she said, "Dad, you're not kidding, are you?" and he said, "NO! THIS IS FOR REAL!" Then she was screaming and the team was screaming and the coaches too . . . and we're in a restaurant!

STAN: You ended up winning both showcases, which meant you bid within two hundred fifty dollars of the price of your showcase. Did you know what you were doing, or did you just get lucky?

VICKY: It was pretty much a shot in the dark. I knew that the Viper was an expensive car. I really didn't know how expensive. I tried to look for my husband, but I couldn't see him, but there were these two young guys in the third or fourth row. I have no idea who they were. They were jumping up going, "Ninety thousand! Ninety thousand!" and I'm thinking to myself *That's an awful lot of money. I don't want to say ninety thousand.* And because I didn't have that much time to think about it, I just said, "Eighty-nine five hundred."

STAN: What did you think when Bob said you'd won both showcases?

VICKY: I thought *This is crazy! What's happening here?* I was excited, but
   I'm like *Is this for real?* It was like an out-of-body experience.

Hey, Vicky, it's time to get back into your body, get some stick-shift lessons, and tool around town in that new Viper of yours!

## The End of the Line

I have a bit of sympathy for the last person in line that I interview. Some people feel they haven't got a chance to get on the show because they're last. "Oh, you've probably already chosen the ones you like," I've heard some of them say. Rest assured, that isn't true.

It's sort of like the kid who always gets picked last for the basketball team. He knows he's going to be the last one, he gets discouraged by it, and has given up hope before the selection process has even begun. Okay, okay, so I was that guy growing up. I admit it. (Special effects: Cue the tears.) And because I was that guy, I always spend a little more time with the last person in line to give him or her hope. Truth be told, I have on many occasions picked the last person to be on the show, not because of the fact that they were last, but because they stood out, because their enthusiasm showed through and they acted as confident and happy to be there as the first person in line.

I love people like that, the ones who make the effort. These are winners, both in the *Price Is Right* line, and in life. I'm extremely grateful for those people because it makes me feel as though my hours of interviewing have paid off right to the very end. They didn't give up on themselves or on me.

The last contestant, just like the last guy picked for the team, often turns out to be the one who has the most success. You just can't predict it.

So strictly speaking as a last-picked-for-the-team kinda guy, I ended up sort of "winning" this job, in spite of it all.

When it came to the wonderful world of fortunate employment and fascinating careers, I won the lotto . . . or should I say, the showcase! There isn't a day that goes by that I don't feel as thrilled as an unsuspecting contestant whose name was just called. Truly, in my own way, I've been one of the few lucky people on earth who has been asked to "Come on down!"

# 15

# JUST THE FACTS, MA'AM
## Things You Don't Know About the Show

**RECORDS ARE CONSTANTLY BROKEN** on *The Price Is Right*. It's already the longest-running network game show in television history. Bob Barker has won more Emmys than anyone. But the list of dazzlers goes on and on.

Here are just a few factoids about *The Price Is Right* for you to mull over and distract yourself with as you eat your breakfast cereal, meditate during yoga, or seek a mental focal point during childbirth:

1. More than 20,000 cars have been offered over 35 years.

2. As of this writing, 58,266 contestants have been called to "Come on down."

3. More than 6,500 shows have been taped since day one.

4. The wheel has been spun more than 45,000 times.

5. There have been more than 80 Barker's Beauties.

6. There have been more than 2,145,000 audience members who have seen the show in person.

7. There are 74 games in rotation now.

8. Not including prizes, the show has spent more than $221,800,000 to be produced over 35 years.

9. The highest winner of all time won $183,688 (in the nighttime version).

10. The highest daytime winner of all time won $147,517.

11. The most expensive showcase ever offered was worth $102,000.

12. The largest underbid in history was $101,000 (having bid $1.00, the same bid that won the above showcase).

13. There was 1 airplane given away.

14. There have been more than 72 shows in which all games were won.

15. There have been more than 72 shows in which all games were lost.

16. The most popular bid for contestant's row is $1.00.

17. Two people have passed out after winning.

18. One person has been topless after her tube top dropped on air.

19. Two people have been in the bathroom when asked to "Come on down."

20. The very first game played on the air was "Any Number."

21. *The Price Is Right* has been re-created in 11 countries around the world. They are: England, Mexico, Spain, France, China, the Netherlands, Vietnam, Australia, Portugal, Canada, and Italy.

22. Besides Bob Barker, the producer, Roger Dobkowitz, is the only person on staff to have been with the show since the very first day in 1972.

23. Celebrities who have appeared on the show have included Sammy Davis Jr., Burt Reynolds, David Hasselhoff, Betty White, Meg Ryan, Tyra Banks, Adam Sandler, Lucille Ball, Vanna White (she was a contestant), Jenny Jones, Patricia Neal, Lyle Waggoner, Lee Meriwether, Chuck Norris, and Larry King, to name a few.

24. The closest bid ever in a showcase without getting it on the nose was only $2.00 away from the actual retail price.

25. Only once has there been a showcase bid that was right on the nose.

26. The first shows did not start by asking someone to "Come on down!" but rather had them "Stand up!"

27. There have been more than 13,000 showcases offered.

28. There have been 13 announcers on the show.

29. There are 27 games that have been retired.

30. The first showcase ever won totaled $2,504, which included a Mazda. The contestant's bid was $2,500.

31. There has been only one pricing game that required *two* players, called "Double Bullseye." The bidders had to bid back and forth auction-style until someone got the price of the car correct.

# 16
## WHO LOVES YA, BOBBY?
### What People Say About Bob

Bob's a role model.

He's got a quick wit.

**IF THERE WERE ANY INDICATION** that Bob Barker is loved and appreciated by his fans, it would be illustrated by the descriptions people have of him. Some are unexpected, all are passionate and always fun. I merely asked a whole bunch of people why they loved Bob. They were more than eager to tell me.

So who loves ya, Bobby? Everyone, that's who!

He's got great bone structure.

I love him because my grandma loves him.

He's never had a bad day on the job.

When I see him, it's like being in the presence of genius.

Who knew a man over eighty could be so hot!

We're the same age, but he's got more hair.

*(He shows his bald head.)*

I love him because we're the same age . . . thirty-nine.

He's got great teeth.

He transcends all generations.

He loves animals.

He has the world's best tan.

He's a dreamboat.

He makes dreams come true.

He's got the ladies! Yeah!

I love his great big wheel.

He's a fox.

Because he has bunnies, and I have bunnies too.

Because BOB ROCKS THE HOUSE!

I love Bob because he let me spin the wheel backwards.

*(This guy was on the show years ago and accidentally spun the wheel backward.)*

Because we have something in common . . . our gray hair.

He's the man.

He's had more beautiful women at his fingertips than any man in the world.

Because he beat the crap out of Happy Gilmore.

He makes everybody smile.

I love Bob's microphone. It gets smaller every year.

He's ageless.

He has the best suits.

# 17

# GOING POSTAL
## Remarkable Fan Mail

**It used to be harder** to send mail than it is now. In the old days, you really had to desperately want to say something in order to be heard. To sit down, write a letter, seal it, stamp it, and go to a mailbox was a project to which one needed to devote a substantial amount of time to accomplish. And yet before e-mail was invented, we had our share of letters. People loved to write, and now that e-mail exists, it's a breeze. Thus we've been the recipient of voluminous amounts of correspondence, some venomous and kvetchy, but mostly kind and appreciative. Amazing how technology brings out the best, and the worst, in all of us.

We used to get a lot of prison mail with photos of inmates declaring their undying love for the models. "When I get out, I'm gonna marry you!" was a common pronouncement to many a Barker Beauty. Some of the pictures that were sent along with the inmates' letters, you wouldn't want to see. As persistent as these guys were, no vows were ever exchanged (as far as I know).

CBS forwards a lot of e-mails to us, and our office manager, Tiffany Bors, goes through all the fan mail, and occasionally hands me some of the more unusual correspondence concerning someone's appearance on the show, in addition to comments or questions about music or showcases.

One of my favorite letters that was actually sent by snail-mail was from a woman who just gushed over Bob and how much she loved watching the show with her elderly grandmother. Her grandmother couldn't get over how handsome Bob is, and the show made both her and her grandmother deliriously happy. So happy, as a matter of fact, that she decided to send a photo of herself and her grandmother as a token of her appreciation and gratitude for years of pleasurable watching. Nothing better than a family photo, I always say. Unless, of course, it's a dead family photo. Yes, the woman sent a picture of herself standing next to her grandmother's open casket, family gleefully perched around the coffin as if it were a dining room table, with smiles on their faces, and Grandma looking as . . . uh, happy, as she could inside that mahogany box. I know that our demographic has skewed older on occasion, but a Nielsen ratings booster this wasn't.

Another letter, sent on a "Happy Easter" card, was from a woman who decided that Bob was going to marry her, and she gave explicit instructions on what he was to do. He was to take the train to Nebraska, meet her at the station, and they would dine right there at the station's restaurant on salad and lasagna as they discussed their future together. Then a house with a picket fence and a yet-to-be-determined dog would await them only a few miles away.

Another lady decided that Bob should buy her a house, but not too big, though. She was extremely specific about what she wanted: just an acre of land with a lovely four-bedroom three-bath cottage, no more than two thousand square feet, as she was willing to compromise just this once. You see, she had larger houses in the past, but didn't want to appear selfish or greedy. She even sent newspaper real estate clippings with circles around various homes to indicate which properties were acceptable to her.

*Office manager Tiffany Bors is buried daily in fan mail that ranges from paper "Plinko" boards, picture requests, and offers of marriage for Bob.*

Regardless of the unusual messages of these folks, there are those letters that are really kind and touching.

Like the letter from the EMS captain who appeared on our show after 9/11 when we did a tribute to firefighters, medics, and police.

*Mr. Barker,*

*I have been intending to write this email for quite some time, however, I am a big procrastinator. I was invited to your show in 2002 with the firefighters and medics from the Washington D.C. area that served at the Pentagon on 9/11/01. It was truly an honor and a privilege to have been a part of that event. Your people really "rolled out the red carpet" for us. For me, that trip had a deeper meaning because it allowed me to meet my father, who at that time lived in Compton, California. My mother and father divorced probably before I was a year old, so I never met my dad until 2002 at the age of 38. It was a surreal reunion, but not as I envisioned. He was 70 years old and an invalid. I had questions, but decided not to ask. Somehow, my questions seemed trivial. After that, we kept in touch until he died in 2004.*

*It is funny how God can take a tragedy such as 9/11 and make something good out of it. Anyway, when I saw that you were retiring soon, I figured that I better write this before I procrastinate another four years. I really cannot express how much I appreciate you inviting us to the show. One of my prayers was to meet my dad before one of us passed away, and God used you to answer that prayer.*

*Take care, and God bless.*

*Alan G. Dorn*
*EMS Captain*
*Arlington County Fire Department*
*Arlington, Virginia*

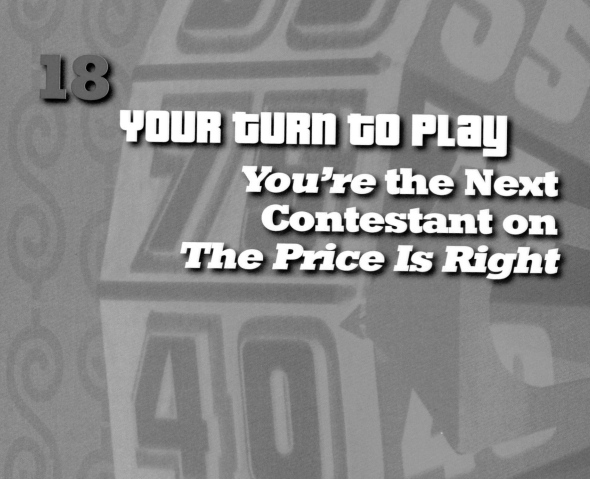

# 18

# YOUR TURN TO PLAY

## *You're the Next Contestant on The Price Is Right*

**OKAY, SMARTY PANTS.** So you think this is easy? You think you'd go home having made a killing if you graced the *Price Is Right* stage with your skilled brilliance? Well, let's see how well you'd do if I picked *you* to "Come on down!" Here's your chance to get up on your dining room table and pretend it's a stage. Wait, forget that idea.

I don't want any chandelier prints in your forehead. Just jump around your living room and pretend you're in the Bob Barker Studio at CBS Television City in Hollywood. I'll be the host, since I've never had the opportunity before, and there isn't a snowball's chance I'll ever do it for real. For purposes of your convenience, the format may be tweaked a bit from the actual show, and the prize copy will be a bit more, let's say, irreverent. Most prices are based on actual retail prices that we've used on the real show.

Let's be crystal clear that this is *my* version of the show ... You're not going to hear this stuff on the air unless the show suddenly goes cable. It's not to be taken too seriously, folks, but I know you'll have fun.

Are you adequately stoked? Are you feeling the tension? Here goes! Now, close your eyes, and pretend that we just came out of a commercial. The screen is dark and you'll be opening your eyes slowly in a moment as if we're fading up from black. Ready, go!

# ACT I

*(Applause!)*

ANNOUNCER: Here it comes! From your magnificent living room! Television's most exciting few minutes of fantastic prizes! It's the fabulous thirty-two-page *Price Is Right*!"

Pixie Prudence, come on down!
*(Cheer!)*

Flossie Farnsworth, come on down!
*(Cheer!)*

Thaddeus Thornhopper, come on down!
*(Cheer!)*

And _____
(that's YOU, genius!), come on down!
*(Big cheer!)*

You are the first four contestants on . . . *The Price Is Right*! And now, here's the star of *The Price Is Right*, Stan!
*(Uproarious applause and standing ovation!)*

STAN: Welcome to *The Price Is Right*! Thank you for joining us. Would someone tell the neighbors to please turn down their stereo? Thanks. Here's the first item up for bid on *The Price Is Right*.

ANNOUNCER: It's a pair of Personal Digital Assistants! *(Applause)* These handy PDAs from BlackBerry are a joy to own, a personal crutch for your social life, and particularly obnoxious when used while having lunch with a troubled friend who is pouring her guts out to you . . . okay, Stan.

STAN: Thank you, Announcer Guy. Okay, Pixie, what do you bid?

PIXIE: I bid $250, Stan.

FLOSSIE: I bid $1,200.

THADDEUS: I bid $2,000.

YOUR bid: _____.

STAN: The actual retail price of the PDA is: _____. *(See answer 1 on page 192.)* *(Applause)*

How did you do? Are you up onstage? Let's assume you are the whiz kid you thought you were and come play the game anyway.

Welcome to the stage, _____ (YOU). You've gotten here at a good time. What's that you say? There's only one thing you want to win? Well, let's see if we can make your dreams come true!

ANNOUNCER: It's a new CAR! *(Applause)* This two-door sporty Mustang convertible comes with automatic transmission, A/C, cloth seats, and no car payments. Perfect for any midlife crisis! Okay, Stan!

STAN: We're going to play "Lucky Seven." I'm giving you seven one-dollar bills (sort of . . . they're printed on the next page). Tell me the numbers in the price of that car, one at a time, and for each dollar you're away from the actual number, you'll lose a dollar (so go get a pencil and cross off the dollars on the page). If you have one dollar left at the end of the game, you can buy that car for one dollar!

# LUCKY $EVEN

2

I'll give you the first number in the price of the car. It's a two.

What's the next number? *(See answer 4 on page 192.)*

Okay, what's the third number? *(See answer 5 on page 192.)*

Tell me the fourth number. *(See answer 8 on page 192.)*

Got any dollars left? Okay, what's the last number?
*(See answer 14 on page 193.)*

Did you win? Okay, whether you did or didn't, get back down in contestant's row and play again. I'm feeling generous today.

## ACT II

STAN: Here's the next item up for bid.

ANNOUNCER: It's an entertaining new electronic keyboard! *(Applause)* From Yamaha, drive the family nuts with your incessant rendition of "When the Saints Go Marching In." This electronic keyboard has features like keys and a board, and it's electronic. How much more do you need to know? . . . Stan.

STAN: Pixie, what do you bid?

PIXIE: Oh . . . I don't know . . . Oh, um, oh . . .

STAN: For God's sake, bid, Pixie! The warranty's almost run out on that keyboard!

PIXIE: Okay, I bid $3,000.

FLOSSIE: I bid $495.

THADDEUS: $1.00, Stan.

YOUR bid: _____.

And the actual retail price of the keyboard is: _____.
*(See answer 3 on page 192.)* *(Applause)*

STAN: You can come up onstage again, because I like you. Yes you, the reader. I'll bet you're excited to be up here again. You are? Well you'll be even more excited if you win this!

ANNOUNCER: A chance to win up to $10,000 dollars in cash! *(Applause)*

STAN: You're going to play "Punch a Bunch." And judging from the desperate look on your face and the fact that you're sitting around doing nothing but playing games in a book, I'm sure you could use the ten grand. I'll give you a chance to punch out four holes on the punchboard. (Once again, get a pencil and cross off the holes on the punchboard opposite . . . don't punch the book, wisenheimer.) But first you'll need to win the punches, so here are some items to price in order to win punches.

ANNOUNCER: It's a portable handheld media player. Enjoy listening to music and watching movies anytime, anywhere, but please not while you're driving or doing my facelift.

STAN: The price says $120. Is it higher or lower than $120? *(See answer 2 on page 192.)*

What's next, Announcer Dude?

ANNOUNCER: Blow your diet with this small ice cream maker with freezer cylinder. No electronics. Just your time, your mess, your recipe, your elbow grease, and your freezer are needed to get something that would taste way better from a store.

STAN: The price says $40. Is it actually higher or lower? *(See answer 6 on page 192.)*

What next, Voice Guy?

ANNOUNCER: It's a ten-cup coffee maker. This coffeemaker makes coffee. What? You were expecting it made bagels maybe?

STAN: It says $30. Higher or lower? *(See answer 11 on page 192.)*

And finally we have what, Copy Crooner?

ANNOUNCER: It's a high-tech shaving system for women. So easy to use, and with this shaver, you'll resent having shaved your legs a lot less when a date stands you up.

STAN: The shaver says $130. Is the actual price higher or lower? *(See answer 15 on page 193.)*

Okay. You've gotten _____ punches on the punchboard. Go and choose your slots and cross them off with your pencil. *(For your results, see answer 20 on page 193.)*

How did you do? Want to try again? Okay, kiddo, hightail it back to contestant's row for another shot.

## ACT III

STAN: What's the next item up for bid?

ANNOUNCER: It's a fun new banjo! *(Applause)* Be the life of the party, or just scare your best friend on a camping trip when you attempt to pluck out the theme to *Deliverance*.

STAN: What do you bid on the banjo, Pixie?

PIXIE: Well, gee, I guess $150.

FLOSSIE: I'll bid . . . ummmmm . . . $800.

THADDEUS: My bid is $801.

YOUR bid: _____.

And the actual retail price of the banjo is: _____.
*(See answer 10 on page 192.)* *(Applause)*

STAN: Come up onstage again, Mr. or Mrs. Reader. How ya feelin'? Ya feelin' confident? Ya feelin' sassy? Ya feelin' like winning this?

ANNOUNCER: It's a new big-screen TV! *(Applause)* This sixty-five-inch rear projection TV from Mitsubishi will be the end of your marriage, but at least you'll have plenty of friends during sporting events.

STAN: You're going to play "Squeeze Play." There are five numbers up on that board. The first number, three, is correct. The last number, eight, is also correct. Either the first nine, the five, or the second nine is *not* correct. You'll need to remove one number. The remaining numbers will squeeeeeeze together to reveal the price. Okay, pick a number and remove it . . . uh, imagine it gone. (No ripping of pages here, folks.) *(See answer 7 on page 192.)*

**SQUEEZE PLAY**

**3 9 5 9 8**

## THE BIG WHEEL

STAN: It's right about here that we'd have a wheel to spin, but since we couldn't fit a three-thousand-pound wheel into this book due to shipping restrictions, we'll just assume you spun well and move on to the next three pricing games. Get back down in contestant's row.

## ACT IV

STAN: Okay, Pronunciation Prince, what is the next item up for bid?

ANNOUNCER: It's a new set of luggage! *(Applause)* Get a really good look at this lovely five-piece set of soft-sided luggage from American Tourister, because it's most likely the last time you'll ever see it after you check it in at the average airport . . . Stan.

STAN: All righty then. Pixie, it's your bid on the luggage.

PIXIE: I bid $700.

FLOSSIE: I just want to say hello to each and every one of my thirty-two foster kids starting with Bennie and Sally and . . .

STAN: Bid!

FLOSSIE: Oh, okay, I bid $1,562.

THADDEUS: What were the other bids, Stan?

STAN: Oy—$700 and $1562.

THADDEUS: Okay, I'll bid $2,550.

YOUR bid: _____.

STAN: And the actual retail price of the luggage is: _____. *(See answer 16 on page 193.)* *(Applause)*
    I know, I know, you're back up onstage again. Ah, the magic of the literary world. And the good news is that you could win this . . .

ANNOUNCER: It's a new truck! *(Applause)* It's a Dodge Dakota, and it comes with standard equipment plus air conditioning and fifteen-inch custom wheels. This truck just screams to all your friends, "Let me help you schlep furniture next time you move!"

STAN: We're going to play "That's Too Much!" I'm going to show you a series of prices for that truck, one at a time. Turn each page, and the minute you see a price that is higher than the actual retail price of that truck, I want you to say, "That's too much!" NO PEEKING AHEAD, AND NO TURNING BACK, BECAUSE IT WRECKS THE GAME, OKAY? Now I don't want you to say "That's too much" with a little wimpy-gimpy voice. I want you to stand in the hallway of your apartment complex, jut out your chest, and shout it like a flea market shopper who just saw an outrageous price for a set of used luggage that someone recently won on a game show! I want you to say it with authority! With vim, vigor, and vitality! I want you to yell, "THAT'S TOO MUCH!" Okay? Okay. Here's the first price.

# $11,980

Do you want to go on? *(Whenever you're ready to stop, see answer 18 on page 193. Otherwise just keep going.)*

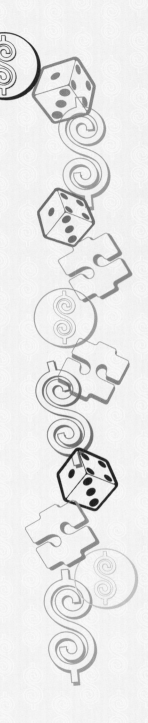

# $13,860

How do you feel about that one?

# $16,582

Done yet?

COME ON DOWN!

# $19,250

How about it?

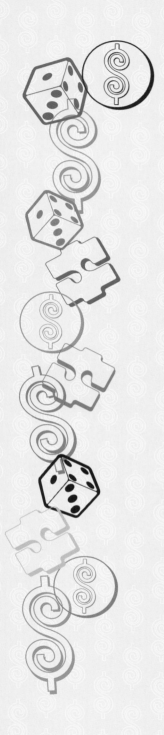

# $20,442

Thinking . . . thinking . . .

# $22,155

Are your knees shaking yet?

# $25,790

The audience is going wild! Are they right?

# $30,456

That's the end of the line, my friend.
*(See answer 18 on page 193.)*

Hey, Reader, if you didn't get it right, you'll have another chance to win something else, so go back down to contestant's row and let's do it again. (You're a lucky person, really. No one on the real show gets to play this many games!)

## ACT V

STAN: Here's our next item up for bid.

ANNOUNCER: It's a new home gym! *(Applause)* Our offering you this space-saving, multi-station home gym complete with weight bench and 160-pound weight stack is no reflection on what kind of shape we think you are in. Though it will make a lovely addition to any bedroom as a clothing caddy and plant hanger for those of you who think driving to the corner to buy beer is exercise.

STAN: Pixie! What's your bid?

PIXIE: I didn't see what it was. What was it?

STAN: Doesn't matter. Just pick a number between one and five thousand.

PIXIE: $5,500.

STAN: Again, oy. Flossie, what do you bid?

FLOSSIE: I bid $4,100.

THADDEUS: I'll say . . . uh, $4,101.

STAN: Ooooooo, the ol' one-dollar-over-the-last-bid trick again. That's wicked. Flossie, don't smack Thaddeus like that. Okay, Reader, your bid.

YOUR bid _____.

STAN: And the actual retail price is: _____.
*(See answer 13 on page 192.) (Applause)*
    Another chance for you to have some fun, Reader. And what kind of fun am I talking about? I'm talking about the kind of fun you can have five inches off the ground . . . on this!

ANNOUNCER: It's a new hovercraft! *(Applause)* This fun vehicle will put your trust in modern technology to the test, as you dash over crocodile-laden swamps and plunge into sand traps at breakneck speeds! It's whip-lash-o-rific!

STAN: You're going to play "Range Game." The price of that hovercraft is quite high. It's somewhere between $15,500 and $16,100. In a moment you're going to move the range finder slowly up the scale. I suggest you pull something out of your wallet or purse at this point, like a card or matchbook to act as a makeshift range finder. Even your two fingers put together would be okay. Put it beside the scale on the page, and slowly move it up the scale alongside the prices. As soon as you see the price within the area of, well, your fingers (or whatever you use), stop. If the price is within that area, get out your neck brace and your attorney's business card, because you'll be driving that hovercraft!

Are you ready? Okay, go. Slowly move up the scale. There you go. (Make a *beep beep beep* sound with your voice, because we have that on the real show and it's way cooler than silence.)

Okay, you've stopped. (*See answer 17 on page 193.*) Good luck!

Did you win? All right. We're giving you one more shot at it, and after essentially being the only real contestant on this show, you should have won *something* by now. Contestant's row beckons you again!

## ACT VI

STAN: What's our final One Bid, Announcer Chap?

ANNOUNCER: Why, it's a portable navigation system! (*Applause*) From Magellan, this GPS system is a real friend when you're lost. And if you're a man, it truly speaks for you by saying, "I don't know where the hell I am and I'm too awesomely masculine to ever ask anyone for directions."

STAN: Pixie, it's your final chance. You've all been in contestant's row for the entire show, so you better get with it!

PIXIE: Of course we've been stuck down here the whole time. You keep giving the win to that person up there staring down at us in this book!

STAN: Bid, Pixie!

PIXIE: $1.00.

FLOSSIE: $179.

THADDEUS: $6,000.

STAN: And they wonder why they've been down there this whole time . . . sheesh. Okay, Reader, what do you bid?

YOUR bid: _____.

STAN: And the actual retail price of the GPS system is: _____. (*See answer 9 on page 192.*) (*Applause*)

Well, what a wonderful surprise to see you here again. Great! And where are you from? (C'mon, say where you're from!) Great! It's really beautiful there this

time of year. And once again, your timing is impeccable, because when you go back to (wherever you just told me) you could be driving in this!

ANNOUNCER: It's a new minivan! *(Applause)* It's a Dodge Caravan SE. It comes with standard equipment plus metallic paint, rear window defroster, radio with cassette and CD player, side curtain airbags, power adjustable pedal, front and rear floor mats, engine block heater, and paint and fabric protection. When you're finished waving good-bye to your fun car and your freedom, dry your tears and hop into this sexy ol' thing. Just add kids and a disguise!

STAN: You're going to play "Card Game." (I suggest you get a deck of cards at this point, or it sort of loses the impact of this game. Actually, it's impossible to play without them, so go get the cards for sure. I know you have a deck because I saw you lose your shirt in "Go Fish" last week.) The object of this game is to get the price of the minivan within $2,000 without going over. You'll draw cards from your deck to bid. Face cards are worth $1,000, and numbered cards are worth that number in hundreds (for instance, a three of clubs would be worth $300, a five of hearts would be $500). Aces are wild. You can make them anything you want. You can keep drawing as long as you want to increase your bid, but don't go over the price of the minivan. We'll start you off with a bid of $10,000 to make it easier.

YOUR TURN TO PLAY!

Ready . . . start pulling cards. Okay, add that to the $10,000. Keep pulling cards if you want. Add each card to the previous one. Are you there yet? Are you going on, or stopping? Remember, you have to be within $2,000 without going over to win the minivan. *(See answer 12 on page 192.)*

## THE BIG WHEEL

STAN: I hope you won, but even if you didn't, we'll pretend you did, which also means you can pretend that you're spinning the wheel. Go ahead and spin!

*(Beep, beep, beep, beep, beep, beep, beep, beep.)*

Wow, Reader! Look! You got a dollar on the wheel, which means you get $1,000 and a bonus spin! Green section gets $5,000, and another dollar gets $10,000 in the bonus spin for a total of $11,000. So go ahead and spin.

*(Beep, beep, beep, beep, beep, beep, beep, beep. . . .)*

Oh my god! You got $10,000! Congratulations. Not only that, but you'll be in the showcase, right after this message.
(Ahhhh, if only it were that easy.)

## SHOWCASES

STAN: We're back, and we're ready to see the showcases. Reader, you're the top winner today (duh, you played six games), and Flossie, you're the runner-up because we needed one. Each of you will have a showcase of fine prizes on which to bid, and, Reader, after seeing your

showcase, you may either bid on it, or pass it to Flossie. The one who comes closer to the actual retail price of your own showcase without going over wins that showcase, and if you're the winner and you're within $250 of your own showcase, you win *both* showcases! Flossie, are you ready?

FLOSSIE: Yes, and I'd also like to say, Stan, that you're the most awesome host ever, and I idolize you.

STAN: Thank you, Flossie. Reader, are you ready? (Say yes.) Okay, you two. Here is the first showcase!

ANNOUNCER: This showcase starts with this beautiful LIVING ROOM! *(Applause)* Presenting this lovely sectional, made of quality fabrics that you'll have a heck of a time matching to your current décor, but don't complain, 'cause it's free.

Plus a lovely TABLE GROUP. *(Applause)* This lovely collection, including a coffee table and two end tables with leaf carvings on the resin legs, has unmistakable French and Italian touches and recalls the interiors of living rooms you've seen at friends' houses in which you've thought, "What were they thinking?"

And new CARPETING . . . *(Applause)* From Schmutzville Carpet Mills, fifty-five square yards of lush, durable carpeting in a dark, dark, stain-proof, no-one-will-see-what-a-bad-housekeeper-I-am brown, designed for style and made for laziness.

And you can add color to your living room with these beautiful FLOWERS FOR A YEAR! *(Applause)* A full year of flowers, one every month, will make any occasion forgivable, whether a fight or a drunken stupor. Your spouse will say, "Thanks, honey, for trying to use a plant as a way to compensate for your dreadful shortcomings."

And sit and relax to the sounds of this elegant BABY

GRAND PIANO! *(Applause)* From Wurlitzer, this beautiful dust collector will bring memories to your home. With its classical design and gorgeous tone, it will remind you every minute of every day that you never reached your full creative potential.

And this showcase can be yours if the Price Is Right!

STAN: Okay, Reader, do you want to bid, or pass on that showcase? Big surprise. You're passing. Okay, Flossie, what do you bid on that showcase?

FLOSSIE: I bid $18,500.

STAN: Okay, Reader, here's your showcase.

ANNOUNCER: Your showcase pays a visit to the world's worst publishing house, Hack & Dreck Publishing. And as it turns out, our editor, Sarah Syntax, is working on a sure-to-fail book called *Harley and Me*, which is about an obsessive relationship between a guy and his unruly new . . . MOTORCYCLE! *(Applause)* From Harley-Davidson, this loud, peace-destroying, awesome rocket has an air-cooled 883cc engine and five-speed transmission. There goes the neighborhood, as you rev it up and join your new leather-clad friends on this incredible machine.

Next, Sarah's working on a truly forgettable novel called *The Pursuit of Crappyness*, which centers on a gentleman desperately attempting to escape the trappings of paradise and move into the slums by trying to flee beautiful . . . KAUAI! *(Applause)* You and a guest will fly round-trip coach for a five-night stay at the Kauai Marriott Resort. Enjoy the land of poi, luaus, and four-figure dinner checks. Get out that equity line of credit, 'cause we're not paying for food!

Finally, we think a true flop will be this latest literary work, *Tequila Mockingbird*, which is a book about a mis-

chievous bird that spends all its time flying around the marina and drinking out of people's margarita glasses while onboard a brand-new festive . . . PARTY BOAT! *(Applause)* This giant sixteen-foot glorified pool raft with two pontoons, a canopy, and a blender-size electric motor will be the talk of the marina. You can just hear the fun and laughter already . . . of the huge cabin cruisers passing by as they point and watch you bobble around in their four-foot wakes.

And this showcase, in which we find that Sarah Syntax has finally found the consummate brilliant literary work of the century called *Come on Down! Behind the Big Doors at* The Price Is Right, can be yours if the Price Is Right!

STAN: Okay, Reader. Add up what you just saw and give me a bid.

YOUR bid: _____.

We'll let you know who the winner is after this short break.

*(Morbid commercial for a mortuary here. Go get a beer and some chips.)*

STAN: Okay, we're back! Flossie, your bid was $18,500. The actual retail price of your showcase is . . . $25,400, for a difference of . . . $6,900.

Reader, you must be closer than $6,900 without going over to win your showcase.

YOUR bid is _____. The actual retail price of your showcase is: _____. *(See answer 19 on page 193.)*

How did you do? I hope you won your showcase, or even both showcases! If you did, the IRS should be sitting outside on your front lawn just about now with a black hooded robe and a scythe.

Thank you all for joining us today on *The Price Is Right*.

This is Stan, reminding you to help control the pet population. Have your pet spayed or neutered. Good-bye, everybody!

*(Hum the theme music, and then close your eyes slowly as we fade to black.)*

COME ON DOWN!

# Answers to Games

**1.** First One Bid: Pair of PDAs—$798

**2.** "Punch a Bunch":  Media player—$95, Lower

**3.** Second One Bid: Electronic keyboard—$1,295

**4.** "Lucky 7": Second number 7

**5.** "Lucky 7": Third number 8

**6.** "Punch a Bunch": Ice cream maker—$29, Lower

**7.** "Squeeze Play": Big-screen TV—Remove #5, Price: $3,998

**8.** "Lucky 7": Fourth number 3

**9.** Sixth One Bid: Navigation system—$1,100

**10.** Third One Bid: Banjo—$1,259

**11.** "Punch a Bunch": Coffeemaker—$40, Higher

**12.** "Card Game": Minivan—$21,264

**13.** Fifth One Bid: Home gym—$2,899

**14.** "Lucky 7": Fifth number 4

**15.** "Punch a Bunch": Shaving system—$114, Lower

**16.** Fourth One Bid: Luggage—$1,200

**17.** "Range Game": Hovercraft—$15,815

**18.** "That's Too Much": Stop at $22,155 (truck is $21,850)

**19.** Showcase 2: $35,506

**20.** "Punch a Bunch":

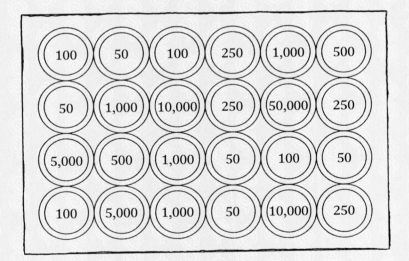

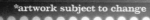